# BY THE
# SKIN OF HIS TEETH

# BY THE
# SKIN OF HIS TEETH

### *The Story of*
### *Thomas Durham: Pioneer, Musician*

## PAUL D. DURHAM

### Editor

PLANTING STICK PRESS

SANDY, UTAH

Durham, Paul Denis, 1949-
By the skin of his teeth: the story of Thomas Durham: pioneer, musician / Paul
D. Durham, editor.
ISBN 978-0-615-35762-1
1. Durham, Thomas. 2. Mormons—Utah—Biography. 3. Utah—Biography. 4.
Pioneers—Utah—Biography. 5. Polygamy—Utah. 6. Musicians—Utah—
Biography.


Printed in the United States of America

⌐ Planting Stick Press
Sandy, Utah

# CONTENTS

# PREFACE

Joseph Campbell writes that a hero has a thousand faces.[1] From studying many of the Willie and Martin handcart company accounts, I know that the hero has at least a thousand faces. That's about how many faces made up the Willie and Martin handcart companies who completed the western migration in 1856. In my mind I didn't really get the chance to put a real image with one of those faces until around 1978. That's when I was shown an original photograph of Thomas Durham. At that time I received a distinct impression that something special and extraordinary was going on with this ordinary British immigrant with humble beginnings.

There has been much praise about this collection of men, women and children, especially some of the individual stories. But in my estimation this has not been hyperbole. There were many who made the transcontinental trek in the nineteenth century. For some it was arduous and life-changing; for others, several accounts state that the journey was without considerable concern and to some degree was enjoyable: the anticipation and expectation of a new life in the American West held such great promise. Some 70,000 Mormon immigrants made that journey across the plains. Most came by covered wagon, the like of which we have seen memorialized in

---

1 Joseph Campbell, *The Hero with a Thousand Faces* (Novato, CA: New World, 2008), Bolingenen Series XVII, 3rd Edition.

cinema and history book. For those in ten other companies who crossed the Great Plains—pulling, pushing, or riding a 160-pound cart filled with maybe 300 pounds of everything they owned—*they* are my heroes.

This is one of those accounts that shouldn't be forgotten, stacked away in some drawer where it won't be seen or read. It's not lengthy, but it has some great value and is a little glimpse into that window of the past that keeps being pushed back into deeper obscurity with each passing generation.

Campbell beautifully illustrates the hero's journey, that universal motif of adventure and transformation in myth and history. Some of his themes explore myth and dream, the call to adventure, the crossing of thresholds, the magic flight, the road of trials, and the hero as saint. On so many levels the experiences of this group of erstwhile pioneers live out these very themes, not as myth, but as reality. Thomas Durham's life is truly representative of the hero. He was one of a thousand and this particular hero is one of a thousand faces. His own call to adventure to leave his native land, a magic flight from inequalities of the Industrial Revolution across the great divide, the unbelievable road of trials for himself and his companions, and the quiet resolve to live peacefully as a Latter-day Saint is unique to him and yet universal to these thousand faces.

Having researched a small fragment of history, I now have a greater respect for a small band of pioneers and the impact that they still can have on this and future generations.

# INTRODUCTION

A young man makes a decision of great importance to himself and to his wife: to leave the land of their ancestors and family and go to another land, a land of opportunity to begin a fresh existence, and another land of refuge for his new-found religion. They are headed to America and leaving the environment of the greatest cotton-spinning industry in the world, located in Lancashire, England in the nineteenth century. As if it were straight out of a Dickens novel, young Thomas Durham, who began working at the age of eleven, spent early years turning spools for one of the big cotton factories in the world's first industrialized city, Manchester. He had come in contact with elders of the Church of Jesus Christ of Latter-day Saints (Mormon) which, between 1837 and 1841 had converted over 5,000 people to the faith. After an expansion of their efforts and the establishment of an organized presence in the British Isles, at least 50,000 members eventually immigrated to America.

Before leaving England, a Mormon elder pronounced a blessing on Thomas with the promise that he would "go to Zion but it will be as by the skin of your teeth." Knowing that he had a destiny to fulfill in a far-off land, he left England in 1856 with his wife and his wife's sister, against the demands of his parents who could not accept this new, American religion. They traveled with fellow saints by sea to Boston and then by rail to as far as they could go west—Iowa City. Due to economic reasons there were a number of companies headed to the Rocky Mountains that could not afford the luxury of covered wagons pulled by oxen. It had been planned in advance that greater numbers could afford the trip if smaller, lighter transportation could be utilized instead of larger, more expensive assemblies.

Handcarts had been designed to make this 1300 mile trip by foot possible. Three companies that year had already departed and would make their way to the Salt Lake Valley without incident. Because of the late arrival of Durham's group and the one just preceding his, many had warned these last two companies that it was too late in the season for them to leave without running into severe weather. These were the Willie and Martin handcart companies. It was well known that playing chance with the weather so late in the season was a great risk; the reports of the Donner Party which became delayed in Utah and then snowbound in the Sierra Nevadas in the winter of 1846-47 emphasized the danger.

Thomas was part of the Martin Company and they started out in late July. It proved to be a mistake of enormous consequence. Of the 576 in the company, it has been estimated that between 103 and 150 people lost their lives. The Willie Company lost seventy-four. Wallace Stegner emphasizes "if courage and endurance make a story, if human kindness and helpfulness and brotherly love in the midst of raw horror are worth recording, this half-forgotten episode of the Mormon migration is one of the great tales of the West and of America."[1] He also writes that "For every early Saint, crossing the plains to Zion in the Valleys of the Mountains was not merely a journey but a rite of passage, the final, devoted, enduring act that brought one into the Kingdom. Until the railroad made the journey too easy, and until new generations born in the valley began to outnumber the immigrant Saints, the shared experience of the trail was a bond that reinforced the

---

[1] Wallace Stegner, "The Mormon Trek: Ordeal by Handcart," *Colliers*, July 6, 1956, 78-85.

bonds of faith; and to successive generations who did not personally experience it, it has continued to have sanctity as legend and myth."[2]

This is Thomas Durham's story (1828-1909). It's a compelling story of how he triumphed over hardship, came to a new land, established a settlement in a new territory, turned into a renowned musician and teacher, local businessman and church leader, as well as a devoted husband and father and raised an educated and well-respected family.

The first section of his story is told by his son, Alfred. Written in 1936 for the Daughters of Utah Pioneers, it is a brief sketch of his life, learned from first-hand telling of stories and reminisces. I have edited it to add information and background to give it a more complete picture.

The second section is Thomas Durham's personal journal which was written by his own hand beginning in 1854 and ending in 1871 and is a significant contribution to his thinking and feelings about his life and times. Of course, it would be better if it were more complete— or if he had written more. But I am grateful for what it is and for what it does and does not contain. The journal commences when young Thomas is twenty-six years old. Some of the entries are very brief, while others are poignant because they are so succinct. When he pens that a very heavy hail storm hit and the river was so high and cold and "it was all I could do to stand it," one can begin to imagine how it might have been. If an entry only says "stayed there 5 days," one can get the sense that we are lucky to even get that entry. When he had

---

[2] Wallace Stegner, *The Gathering of Zion: The Story of the Mormon Trail* (Lincoln and London: University of Nebraska Press, 1992), 1.

only mustered sufficient strength to write that brief description, the horrific circumstances can only be imagined and reconfirmed by other eyewitness accounts. Along with former Church Historian G. Homer Durham's commentaries added in 1963 and 1966, I have annotated this account to make it more comprehensive.

I hope that his account can now stand alongside those of so many other wonderful and courageous pioneer men and women.

Paul Denis Durham
Salt Lake City, Utah
March 2010

# SKETCH OF THE LIFE OF

# THOMAS DURHAM

## (1828-1909)

By Alfred M. Durham[1]

Edited by Paul Denis Durham

---

[1] This paper was prepared by Alfred Morton Durham (1872-1957), third child of Thomas and Caroline Mortensen Durham (1850-1915), in Salt Lake City, Utah, for "Camp Seventeen," Daughters of Utah Pioneers, October 7, 1936. Alfred M. Durham, Julliard School-educated musician, teacher, educator, state legislator, and missionary to Tonga, known for his organ playing and hymn writing. He composed the music to "They, the Builders of the Nation," *Hymns* (Salt Lake City: The Church of Jesus Christ of Latter-day Saints, 1985), no. 36, "Again, Our Dear Redeeming Lord," (*Hymns*, 1985, no. 179) and in 1930 the spirited anthem written for the youth of the church: "Carry On," (*Hymns*, 1985, no. 255) which catchphrase President Gordon B. Hinckley announced would be the theme for his new administration. See Jeffrey R. Holland, "President Gordon B. Hinckley: Stalwart and Brave He Stands," *Ensign*, June 1995, 2-13. Some records have shown the subject's full name as Thomas Washington Durham, but no direct confirmation has been substantiated and there is no mention of a middle name in his diary written in his own hand. The death certificate filled out by his son requiring a full name shows no middle name. See State of Utah, Div. of Archives and Records Service http:// archives.state.ut.us/cgibin/indexesresults.cgi?RUNWHAT=IDXFILES&KEYPATH =IDX2 08420020370 (accessed Nov. 20, 2008). It has been edited (2010) by Paul Denis Durham, b. 1949 (great-grandson of Thomas Durham 1828-1909), grandson of Alfred Morton Durham (1872-1957), and son of Alfred Richards Durham (1918-1983). See Alfred M. Durham, "Sketch of the Life of Thomas Durham, prepared for Camp Seventeen, Daughters of Utah Pioneers, Oct. 7, 1936," copy of typewritten manuscript, History Department, International Society Daughters of Utah Pioneers, Salt Lake City, 6 pp. Footnotes have been added by the editor.

T he subject of this sketch was born in Oldham, [Lancashire county] England,[2] on the 2nd day of May, 1828. He was the son of John and Isabella Thompson Durham,[3] there being three other children in the family, a brother and two sisters.[4]

---

[2] Oldham was the center for an agricultural district with a woolen industry until the 19th century, when it became a major cotton-spinning and weaving town. "Although Oldham's existence can be traced back to the 11th century, it was the Industrial Revolution—and cotton in particular—that laid the foundations for the town's prosperity. By the end of the 19th century Oldham was recognized near and far as nothing less than the greatest cotton spinning town in the world." Oldham England, "Town of Oldham England," http://wwp.greenwichmeantime.com/ time-zone/europe/uk/england/oldham/index.htm (accessed Oct. 25, 2008). It wasn't until the American Civil war and the blockade of cotton from the Confederate Southern States by the Union, that there was a significant decline of raw cotton to the mills of England that triggered the decline of the cotton industry (1861-1865) from which it never fully recovered. "The town, which is one of the most important seats of the cotton manufacture in the world, owes its prosperity in great part to its situation on the edge of the Lancashire coal-field, where the mineral is very easily wrought . . . . The total number of persons engaged in the industry is over 30,000, the annual consumption of cotton being over 700,000 bales, or about one-fourth of the whole quantity of cotton imported into the United Kingdom . . . . The population . . . in 1801 had increased to 12,024, in 1841 to 42,595, in 1861 to 72,333 . . . . Although consisting chiefly of monotonous rows of workmen's houses, interspersed with numerous immense factories and workshops, Oldham has some good streets and a number of imposing public buildings." The Encyclopedia Britannica, 9th ed., (Philadelphia: J.M. Stoddart, 1884) s.v. "Oldham," 780-781.

[3] John Durham (b. Dec. 18 1790, Whitby, Yorkshire, England, d. Jan. 10, 1863); Isabella Thompson (b. Jan. 20, 1800, Whitby, Yorkshire, England, d. Mar. 31, 1883). Whitby is an historic town in the Scarborough district of North Yorkshire on the northeast coast of England, facing the North Sea, which dates back to 657 A.D. It is situated 47 miles from York. In 1753 the first whaling ship set sail from Whitby to Greenland and began a new phase in the town's development. "It was here, at the Synod of Whitby in 664 AD, that the Saxon Christians decided to adopt the customs of the Roman Catholic Church instead of the Celtic Church. The council was held in Whitby Abbey, an important monastery founded by St. Hilda, a Saxon princess, in 657 AD. In the centuries that followed, Whitby hosted such notable figures as St. Caedmon (the first English poet), William Scoresby (a whaler featured in *Moby Dick*), Captain James Cook, and Bram Stoker (who set much of *Dracula* in

He was of medium stature, about five feet, eight and one-half inches in height and weighed about 150 to 155 pounds. He had a fair complexion, and had light golden hair until about eighteen years of age when it turned to a jet black of which there was an abundance. He was very athletic as a young man and particularly excelled in the running broad jump and similar events.

He was reared in a God-fearing home, under religious influences, his father and mother giving the children all the advantages they could afford according to their circumstances. One example of his father's good judgment about the smoking habit which was so common at the time may be stated: he said that if the Lord had intended that men should smoke tobacco that he would have provided a little chimney somewhere on the anatomy to take care of the smoke. This is an example of the judgment used in so many ways in the rearing of his family.

While the children were young the family moved to Stalybridge,[5] which became the permanent home of the family. The children were

---

Whitby)." Sacred Destinations, "Whitby." http://www.sacred-destinations.com/england/whitby.htm (accessed Nov. 20, 2008).

[4] The children of John Durham and Isabella Thompson Durham were: Sarah Durham, b. June 6, 1825; Thomas Durham, b. May 2, 1828; John Durham, b. Aug. 22, 1831; Isabella Durham, b. April 3, 1834; Mary Ann Durham, b. Sept. 1, 1836; Elizabeth Durham, b. circa June 24, 1841. See Thomas Durham, Thomas Durham Journal 1854-1871, ed. Paul Denis Durham, typescript, (Sandy, Utah, 2010), 1-2.

[5] Stalybridge, county of Cheshire, is a small town in the north-west of England lying at the foothills of the Pennines, which are also known as the backbone of Britain, 8 miles east of Manchester. In 1831 the population was 14,216 and inhabited houses numbered 2,357. The town of Stalybridge was the creation of the Industrial Revolution. Cotton and the spinning industry lead to the development of Stalybridge as a town. The name Stalybridge originally came about due to the local Manor of Stayley, and the bridge which crossed the River Tame. (Not to be confused with the River Thames.) A song written by Jack Judge and Harry Williams in Stalybridge in

given the usual opportunities for schooling, as afforded in those days, and Thomas was given a liberal education in music under a skillful teacher, a Mr. John Farrington, a man whom my father loved, and often referred to in later life, and which preparation was very valuable in the work he was destined to do in his later life.

He was apprenticed out in his youth, as was the custom, to learn a trade, that of wood turning, and he applied this knowledge for some time in turning the spools for one of the big cotton factories in Manchester,[6] another accomplishment that served him well at a later time.[7]

---

1912, "It's a Long Way to Tipperary," became a marching anthem on the battlefields of Europe. See http://www.stalybridge.org.uk/history.htm (accessed Oct. 25, 2008).

[6] Manchester was in close proximity to Stalybridge, circa eight miles. Historically, most of the city, Manchester, was a part of Lancashire, with areas south of the River Mersey being in Cheshire. It is said that Manchester was the world's first industrialized city and it played a dominant role during the Industrial Revolution. It was the international center of textile manufacture and cotton spinning and received the nickname Cottonopolis. "The transformation from a market town to a major city began in 1761 when the . . . canal began to bring cheap coal to Manchester. By the end of the 18th century Manchester had established itself as the centre of the cotton industry in Lancashire. The merchants brought the raw cotton from Liverpool, sold it to small-time masters in Manchester who then passed it to the spinners working in the cottages. In the 1770s the invention of machines such as the Spinning Jenny and the Water Frame completely changed the way that cotton goods were produced. The machines in the first textile factories were driven by water-power and were therefore built in villages besides fast-flowing streams. By 1790 there were about a hundred and fifty water-powered cotton spinning factories in Britain. Richard Arkwright was quick to see the significance of the Rotary Steam-Engine invented by James Watt and in 1783 he began using the machine in his Cromford factory. Others followed his lead and by 1800 there were over 500 of Watt's machines in Britain's mines and factories. With the invention of Watt's steam-engine, factories no longer had to be built close to fast-flowing rivers and streams. Entrepreneurs now tended to build factories where there was a good supply of labour and coal. Manchester became the obvious place to build textile factories. Large warehouses were also built to store and display the spun yarn and finished cloth. The town's population grew rapidly. With neighbouring Salford, Manchester had about 25,000 inhabitants in 1772. By 1800 the

As a young man, he came in contact with elders of the L.D.S. Church [Church of Jesus Christ of Latter-day Saints] and especially

---

population had grown to 95,000. The rich manufacturers built large houses around the Mosley Street area. At first the cheap housing for the factory workers were confined to New Cross and Newtown. However, as the population grew, close-packed houses were built next to factories all over Manchester." See Medieval British Towns, "Manchester," http://www.spartacus.schoolnet.co.uk/ITmanchester.htm (accessed March 26, 2009). "Despite the growing wealth due to trade and commerce, prosperity lay in the hands of very few of Manchester's residents. The working people, who actually produced the wealth, lived, worked and died in conditions of the most desperate poverty and degradation. Innumerable reports and surveys were carried out during the 19th century, and they all told much the same story: poor wages, impossibly long working hours, dangerous and unsanitary working conditions, even more unsanitary dwellings, little or no health provisions, high infant mortality and a short life expectancy. A map of Manchester showing age of death figures in the mid-nineteenth century revealed that life expectancy was directly related to wealth. Put simply, the poor died younger and the rich lived longer. At that time, Ancoats was the death black spot of Manchester. Records show that by 1830 there were over 560 cotton mills in Lancashire, employing more than 110,000 workers, of which 35,000 were children - some as young as six years of age. Wages for children were about 2s.3d. (two shillings and three pence) per week (about 11½ new pence), but adults were paid about 10 times more. Hence, it made economic sense to employ as many children and as few adults as possible, and this is exactly what happened. Youngest children were employed to crawl beneath machinery (while still in operation) to gather up loose cotton—they were known as 'scavengers' and many died by getting caught up in machinery. Those that survived to adulthood had permanent stoops or were crippled from the prolonged crouching that the job entailed. The typical working day was 14 hours long, but many were much longer, as, without regulation, unscrupulous mill owners could demand any terms they liked." See Manchester UK, "History and Heritage," http://www.manchester2002-uk.com/history.html (accessed March 26, 2009).

[7] His sister, Sarah worked in the Nottingham Cotton and Lace factory. "She told how the lint would get so thick on the floor that they would take buckets of water to wash it off so they could work." See Emma Topham and Cora Rowley, "A Sketch of the Life of Sarah Durham Morris as Remembered by her Grandaughters," [sic] (Cedar City, UT, n.p., n.d., photocopy of typescript ), 81.

with Elder Cyrus H. Wheelock,[8] who was a frequent visitor at the home while fulfilling a mission to England, and also with Joseph Morris[9] who later became the head of the short lived Morrisite branch, but who labored unceasingly with my father to impress him with the gospel message.[10]

---

[8] Cyrus Wheelock was second counselor to Franklin D. Richards (President of the European Mission and member of the Quorum of the Twelve Apostles), and composer of the words to the hymn, "Ye Elders of Israel," *Hymns*, no. 319.

[9] "Joseph Morris, prophet and leader of the Morrisites, was born in 1817 and joined the Church of Jesus Christ of Latter-day Saints when he was twenty-three years old while he was living in England. He married Mary Thorpe and brought her to America, where they resided in St. Louis for two years. Moving to Pittsburgh, Pennsylvania, Joseph became the local Mormon congregation's branch president. Morris and his family immigrated to Utah in 1853 and resided for a time in Sanpete County, subsequently moving to Provo, and then Slaterville, before settling in the small community of South Weber. He claimed to have received numerous spiritual manifestations, but it was in 1857 before he recorded his first official revelation. This revelation established Morris's prophetic calling, placing him at odds with the leadership of the Mormon Church, designated him as the seventh angel of the apocalypse, outlined ten steps to godhood, explained the doctrine of reincarnation, and proclaimed the 'immediate' second coming of Christ. Morris also taught that Brigham Young was a fallen prophet and that no more Mormon missionaries should be sent into the world." Kenneth Godfrey, "The Morrisites," in *Utah History Encyclopedia*, ed. Allan Kent Powell (Salt Lake City: University of Utah Press, 1994), 381-382.

[10] The Church of Jesus Christ of Latter-day Saints had a profound effect on this region of England. "Between 1837 and 1841 there were two apostolic missions to the British Isles. In 1837-1838 Heber C. Kimball and Orson Hyde established the first mission, concentrating in the area of Preston and the Ribble Valley. [Stalybridge is only about 40 miles from Preston. It is claimed that Charles Dickens used the town of Preston as the basis for his novel, *Hard Times*, published in 1856 and named "Coketown" in the novel. He had visited the town for research early in 1856 during a cotton strike which by that time had already been in effect for over twenty weeks.] Their efforts saw about 1,500 people baptized into the Church. From 1839 to 1841, nine members of the Quorum of the Twelve Apostles labored in Britain and added another 4,000 converts to the Church. These missions were extremely important. In a

Father was not hasty to accept the new doctrine, but never doubted its truth, he taking his time to fully satisfy himself before taking the final step which he did, when he became of age, being baptized on the 1st day of May, 1850. He had served as choir leader of the branch, however, for four years previous to his baptism, and continued his work in the branch as branch clerk, choir leader and branch president until he emigrated in 1856.

---

relatively short time, the Twelve Apostles established the foundation for the most successful missionary program of the Church in the nineteenth century, organized an extensive emigration program, and established a major publication program . . . . Elders Kimball and Hyde were in England from July 1837 to April 1838. Landing at Liverpool, they traveled north to Preston, where relatives of Canadian converts provided various assistance, including a place to preach. Finding ready acceptance of their message, they baptized more than 140 people by October 1837. They moved up the Ribble Valley, finding other audiences, particularly among the textile workers throughout Lancashire. By the time they returned home in April 1838, Church membership had grown to about 1,500 people in Britain, in spite of growing opposition, particularly from local clergy . . . . The second apostolic mission was . . . initiated by divine revelation. On July 8, 1838, from the new headquarters at Far West, Missouri, the Prophet Joseph Smith . . . received a revelation that the Twelve Apostles were to leave Far West on . . . on a mission 'over the great waters' (D&C 118:4). Most of the members of the Twelve made their way in various groups to Liverpool. By April 1840, they were together for the first time as a quorum in a foreign land. On April 14, 1840, in Preston, they ordained Willard Richards an apostle and sustained Brigham Young as 'standing president' of their quorum . . . . They separated to various assigned geographical areas: Brigham Young and Willard Richards were to assist Wilford Woodruff with the work he had already begun among the United Brethren in Herefordshire; Heber C. Kimball was to return to the areas of his 1837-1838 missionary successes; Parley P. Pratt was to establish a mission home and publishing concern in Manchester; Orson Pratt was assigned to Scotland, where the work had already begun; John Taylor was to go to Liverpool, Ireland, and the Isle of Man; and George A. Smith would extend their work to London. Their effort [resulted in] . . . the establishment of a successful emigration program that saw the first converts gathered to Nauvoo, with at least 50,000 members emigrating from the British Isles to America." David J. Whittaker and James R. Moss, "Missions of the Twelve to the British Isles," *Encyclopedia of Mormonism*, ed. Daniel H. Ludlow (New York: Macmillan, 1992), 920-921.

About 1852, he married Mary Morton,[11] a woman of ability and refinement and a wife and companion of whom any man could be proud, and a member of the church as well so that they had interests in common in every way.

Before leaving England, Elder Wheelock gave Father a blessing and among other things said: "You will go to Zion but it will be as by the skin of your teeth; and when you get there, the Angels of Heaven will sing to you and give you music as you sleep, and you will be able to write it and sing it in the Temples of our God." The fulfillment of the prediction will be noted a little later in this narrative.

With his wife and his wife's sister Eliza,[12] whose father and mother were both dead, he left England in May 1856 bound for Zion, his own father and mother pleading with him not to leave England and them for this new religion which they could not accept and which they never did receive in mortal life, outside of his one sister Sarah who was all ready a member and who later came to Utah and lived and died a devout member of the church. "Two of a family" so we find in holy writ,[13] and so it was with this family.[14]

---

[11] Mary Morton, b. Jan. 30, 1829 at Staylybridge, Lancashire to Joshua (1803-1835) and Harriet Morton. Thomas actually married Mary on Oct. 22, 1849 "at Hollinwood, near Oldham, Lancashire in the presence of [his] sister Sarah and her husband & others." See Thomas Durham Journal 1854-1871, in this volume, p. 49. Mary Morton Durham had no children. She is the author of a number of hymns including "Sweet Is the Peace the Gospel Brings," (Hymns, 1985, no. 14). This editor has found no evidence of a middle name, Ann.

[12] Eliza Morton, (b. Nov. 23, 1835, Stalybridge, Lancaster, England; d. Dec.12, 1917, Grave location: Mountain View Cemetery, Beaver, UT, Grave C-362-2. See Utah Burials, Utah State History; http://history.utah.gov/apps/burials (accessed Nov. 22, 2009).

[13] "Turn, O backsliding children, saith the Lord; for I am married unto you: and I will take you one of a city, and two of a family, and I will bring you to Zion:" (Jeremiah 3:14)

They had a long, hard sea voyage (eight weeks),[15] and after landing at New York they entrained for Omaha,[16] the season was getting late and the last company of hand carts for that season was being made up preparatory for the westward journey. Some friends of father tried to persuade him to remain over until the next season, offering to help him get work but he had left his all to go to Zion and nothing could dissuade him now to stay even for another year.

---

[14] "The Durhams were a well-to-do influential people in the locality and [the children] could have about the best of everything." Thomas' sister, Sarah, "sacrificed it all for the truths of the Gospel." "She was baptized into the LDS Church in 1844. [Six years prior to his joining the Church.] Her parents were quite opposed to this turn of events and never fully forgave Sarah and her brother Thomas for joining this religion. Sarah used to talk about Bella (her sister, Isabella) quite a bit. Once she wrote back to England imploring Bella to take good care of their parents. Bella replied that she did not have to be reminded of her duty, intimating that it was Sarah herself who was shirking her responsibility because she had come to America and left them. She and Thomas sang in a choir called 'The United Brethren.' This was the name of a religious organization and the story is told that Elder Wilford Woodruff of the LDS Church came to one of their meetings and converted most of the congregation, probably among them Sarah and her brother Thomas." See Topham and Rowley, "A Sketch of the Life of Sarah Durham Morris as Remembered by her Grandaughters," [sic] 81.

[15] Actually, the travel time was just over a month. The ship, *Horizon*, chartered by the church, carried the last large company of Latter-day Saint emigrants from England, and departed Liverpool May 25, 1856 and arrived in Boston on June 28, 1856. During the crossing there were four marriages, four births, and five deaths. See Andrew D. Olsen, *The Price We Paid: The Extraordinary Story of the Willie and Martin Handcart Pioneers* (Salt Lake City: Deseret Book, 2006), 219, 221.

[16] The end of the rail was actually Iowa City, Iowa. After arriving in Boston (not New York), the majority traveled by train for eight days through Albany, Buffalo, Cleveland, Toledo, Chicago and Rock Island, Illinois. They arrived in Iowa City on July 8, 1856, twelve days after the Willie Handcart Company had arrived and both companies were in Iowa City until the Willie Company left on July 15. See Olsen, *The Price We Paid*, 227, 230.

It was the ill-fated Martin Company late in July that started out on that hazardous journey which father joined, and about which so much has been said and written since.[17] Four were assigned to a handcart[18];

---

[17] "The economic impact of the drought and grasshopper infestation on the Mormon community [in the Utah Territory] stretched Church resources to the limit. It was apparent that the funds needed for immigration in 1856 would be totally inadequate. Brigham Young elected to try a plan that had been considered for years but never tried—emigration by handcart." Williams W. Slaughter and Michael Landon, *Trail of Hope: The Story of the Mormon Trail* (Salt Lake City: Shadow Mountain, 1997), 117. "A 'well-finished, ironed and painted' handcart cost $20. A 'more primitive style, and without iron' cost only $10. Wagons averaged $90, and oxen to pull them averaged about $70 a yoke, with three yoke required to pull a full wagon. A wagon outfit, then, could cost $300." Olsen, *The Price We Paid*, 29. "Five handcart companies left Iowa city for the Salt Lake Valley that year [1856]. The first two companies, captained by Edmund Ellsworth and Daniel D. McArthur, made the arduous trip without incident, both arriving in Salt Lake City on September 26. A third smaller company, captained by Edward Bunker and composed primarily of emigrants from Wales, arrived on October 2. The last two handcart companies—The James G. Willie and Edward Martin companies—left late, while winter came early. The members of these two companies and the Hunt and Hodgett wagon trains traveling with them endured one of the most tragic journeys in all of overland emigration history." Slaughter and Landon, *Trail of Hope*, 117. The Martin Company, the season's last and fifth handcart company contained 575 individuals, 145 handcarts, and 8 wagons when it began its journey from the outfitting post at Iowa City, Iowa (departure July 28, 1856; arrival in Salt Lake Valley November 30, 1856.) See "Immigration to Utah," *Deseret News*, Oct. 15, 1856, 254. "In makeup the Willie and Martin companies resembled earlier trains: one-third of the members were children under thirteen, one-third women, one-quarter men, and one percent over sixty-five years. The Martin company was half again as large as other companies; half of its families were headed by widows (much more than half by the time they reached South Pass); and, while there were plenty of bachelors who might have shouldered the loads, many of these included, in Franklin D. Richards's description, "cripples, and old grey-headed men." (*Historian's Office Minutes*, October 4, 1856, Church History Library) as cited in Rebecca Bartholomew and Leonard J. Arrington, *Rescue of the 1856 Handcart Companies* (Signature Books: Salt Lake City, 1993), footnote 8 of the Introduction. "Between 1847 and 1869, some 70,000 members of the Church of Jesus Christ of Latter-day Saints came to Utah by overland trail. Most of them traveled in wagon companies, but approximately 3,000—4 percent of the total—came by handcart. In all, ten companies of handcart

father and wife, his sister-in-law, Eliza, and another woman made up the group for him to look after. They trudged along, making but few miles per day, and wearily making their camp at night. The men had to take turns herding the few cattle they had along on the few wagons that carried a portion of the supplies, this task coming about every other night. Snow fell early in September and the suffering from this time on was too terrible to be described. Father says that he waded rivers and streams day after day with the ice floating down and cutting his bare limbs until they would bleed, making sometimes several trips back and forth, carrying women and children on his back and then

---

pioneers made the journey to Utah between 1856 and 1860. Although pulling handcarts was arduous even in the best of conditions, eight of these companies made the journey more quickly and with fewer deaths than the typical wagon company. The other two handcart companies—the Willie and the Martin Companies—suffered a tragedy that President Gordon B. Hinckley described as 'without parallel in the western migration of our people.'" Olsen, *The Price We Paid*, 3. "Perhaps their suffering seems less dramatic because the handcart pioneers bore it meekly, praising God, instead of fighting for life with the ferocity of animals and eating their dead to keep their own life beating, as both the Fremont and Donner parties did. But if courage and endurance make a story, if human kindness and helpfulness and brotherly love in the midst of raw horror are worth recording, this half-forgotten episode of the Mormon migration is one of the great tales of the West and of America." Wallace Stegner, "The Mormon Trek: Ordeal by Handcart," *Collier's*, July 6, 1956, 78-85.

[18] "According to the handcart plan, the emigrants would pull light-weight two wheeled carts that had shallow boxes on top, about three feet wide by five feet long, for carrying their belongings. Five people would typically be assigned to each cart, and each of them would be allowed 17 pounds of personal belongings. The weight of the handcart itself would be 60 to 75 pounds, so the total weight, with luggage, would generally be about 160 pounds . . . ." Olsen, *The Price We Paid*, 25. "For the Martin company, September's journey across Nebraska was more difficult than August's across Iowa. One reason is that the handcarts were heavier, each loaded with 100 [additional] pounds of flour and some carrying tents." Olsen, *The Price We Paid*, 295.

dragging into camp, making a fire and drying his scanty clothing out, so he could be ready for the ordeal another day. The food became scarce, and they were compelled to be rationed down to four ounces of flour per day for a time, until supplies were sent out from Salt Lake to relieve the suffering. Father said they would mix the pound of flour with a little water each morning, bake the mixture, cut it in four parts, for his group, and that was their supply until the next morning. The snow fell in such quantities that they were compelled to leave much of their personal clothing and effects, in order to make any headway at all, they finally reached Salt Lake City late in November. He related that many times he has gone out after reaching camp, and men who had given up, practically frozen to death, and weary of it all, and has literally dragged them into camp, warmed and revived them and thus saved their lives. He helped to bury many in shallow graves, and assisted in burying as many as fourteen in a single grave at one time; for be it known that about one-third of the company that started out to make this journey died and were buried by the way.[19] Did Father get to Zion as by the skin of his teeth? As predicted by Elder Wheelock?[20]

---

[19] The estimate of total fatalities for both the Willie and Martin companies is between 177 and 224 people, with numerous amputations, frozen limbs, and resulting widows and orphans. The death toll for the Willie is generally recognized at 74 of 500 total people; the sum of the Martin Company varies from 103 to 150 of the total 576 participants. See Slaughter and Landon, *Trail of Hope*, 180. See also Olsen, *The Price We Paid*, 172, 401.

[20] One first-hand account reads, "After our food had given out, we went to our tent to die," Elizabeth Sermon [age 37], Martin company, wrote out on the trail. Her husband had been failing for days. "He put his arm around me," she continued, "and said, 'I am done' and breathed his last. We sewed him up in a quilt with his clothes on, except his boots, which I put on my feet and wore them into Salt Lake City.'" Heidi Swinton and Lee Grosberg, *Sweetwater Rescue: The Willie and Martin Handcart Story* (American Fork: Covenant, 2006), Preface. Another account reads: "In the midst of death and tragedy (Saturday, October 25, 1856), people did what they had to do to stay alive. At some point along the trek, as people were passing

away due to exhaustion, Mettie Kerstena Mortensen, [sister of Caroline Mortensen, the future wife of Thomas Durham] age 11, took a crust of bread from a dead woman's pocket. Although it was surely a justifiable act of survival, she reported that she felt bad about her theft for the rest of her life." Rhoda M. Wood, "Mettie Kerstena Mortensen Rasmussen, wife of Christen Rasmussen," Daughters of Utah Pioneers Library, as cited in Paul D. Lyman, *The Willie Handcart Company* (Provo, Utah: BYU Studies, 2006), 158-159. On October 5, 1856, Brigham Young issued the immediate call to assemble rescue parties from the Salt Lake valley to move as quickly as possible to bring provisions and help to the desperate saints in (present-day) Wyoming. He said, "Many of our brethren and sisters are on the plains with handcarts . . . and they must be brought here, we must send assistance to them . . . . That is my religion; that is the dictation of the Holy Ghost that I possess. It is to save the people . . . to save our brethren that would be apt to perish, or suffer extremely, if we do not send them assistance." *Deseret News*, Oct. 15, 1856, 252, as cited in Olsen, *The Price We Paid*, 116. "On the 28th Joseph A. Young and two companions, with the news of coming supply trains, met them, an event which brought forth 'the cheers and tears and smiles and laughter of the emigrants.' Two days later they met the promised supplies on the Sweetwater near Devil's Gate. This assured relief, but much of suffering had yet to be endured. From a foot to a foot and a half of snow was on the ground and the cold was intense. The question was discussed as to whether the company should go into such winter quarters as could be provided or push on to Salt Lake. The latter course was determined upon. The freight that could not be taken along was left at this point with three men from the valley, and seventeen from among the emigrants to guard it. Only a small allowance of food could be left them, and because of this the men suffered terribly, and nearly perished of hunger by the time spring opened and relief arrived from Salt Lake valley . . . . Shortly after leaving Devil's Gate enough wagons were met to carry most of the baggage of Martin's company and some of the people, but the crossing and recrossing of the Sweetwater was a trying ordeal. There were so many who were helpless, or nearly so, that it was difficult to decide who should be taken into the wagons and who should be compelled to walk. 'There was considerable crying of women and children,' remarks Elder Jacques, 'and perhaps of a few of the men, whom the wagons could not accommodate with a ride.' 'One of the relief party remarked,' continues our authority, 'that in all the mobbings and drivings of the 'Mormons' he had seen nothing like it.' C.[Cyrus] H. Wheelock (who, it will be remembered, was one of the presidency of the British Mission when this enterprise was undertaken, and who was now returned with the relief party to assist these emigrants, also one of the last who was with the Prophet Joseph at Carthage Prison) could scarcely refrain from shedding tears, and he declared that he would willingly give his own life if that would save the lives of the emigrants." See B. H. Roberts, *A*

After remaining in Salt Lake City for a few days and resting up from the long journey, he and his wife and sister-in-law journeyed, with friends, 250 miles farther south to Parowan, Iron County,[21] which had been settled nearly five years before, where they arrived on the 12th of December. This was on Friday and on Sunday Father was asked to take the choir and he led the choir there until his death in March 1909, having been in charge of L.D.S. choir work in England and here over 62 years, I am sure a church record.[22]

---

*History of the Church of Jesus Christ of Latter-day Saints*, Century I, Vol. IV, (Salt Lake City: Deseret News Press, 1930), 98-99.

[21] As the first settlement of southern Utah (settled January, 13, 1851 by a party led by Apostle George A. Smith), Parowan is affectionately called the "Mother Town of Southern Utah." Originally called The City of the Little Salt Lake, it was renamed Parowan (a Piute Indian name meaning "evil water," a designation given to a story about an Indian girl being over-swept by lake waves.) See "Parowan Valley History," Parowan Utah, www.parowan.org/history.html (accessed Nov. 22, 2008). Located ca. 234 miles from Salt Lake City, it is the county seat of Iron County. Thomas Durham served as mayor 1902-1904. "George A. Smith officially named the new location 'Fort Louisa,' in honor of Louisa Beaman, the first documented woman to marry into polygamy among the Latter-day Saints." On May 16, 1852, Brigham Young personally inspected the settlement and officially named it Parowan. See Janet Burton Seegmiller, *A History of Iron County: Community Above Self* (Salt Lake City: Utah State Historical Society [and] Iron County Commission, 1988), 50, 53. "Only three years after the first Mormon pioneers arrived in Salt Lake Valley, a number of them were called to establish an iron works in southern Utah. Like their biblical counterparts, these modern Saints would shortly find themselves undergoing a trial of faith in the furnace of their own desert wilderness." See Morris A. Shirts and Kathryn H. Shirts, *A Trial Furnace: Southern Utah's Iron Mission* (Provo, Utah: Brigham Young University Press, [n.d., 2001?]), xix. The iron industry, producing little pig iron, turned out to be doomed from the beginning and ended in 1858.

[22] "Brigham Young personally called Brother Durham to proceed immediately to Parowan to direct the musical activities there. He arrived at his destination December 12, 1856. Two days later, on a Sunday, he took charge of the Parowan choir and directed it until death fifty three years later in 1909—fifty years of

He secured a home inside the fort, an enclosure built of mud, a wall some four feet in width at the base, and two and a half to three feet at the top and about twelve feet high, and also some farming land both of which are in the possession of members of the family now. And during these first years took his turn in guarding from Indian raids, helped in the erection of a meeting house and other public buildings and took a general interest in community life.[23]

On the approach of Johnston's army in 1857, father was called to go out to the White Mountain country in Nevada[24] to find a hiding place for the people in case it became necessary for them to leave their homes. The company spent some six months out in the vicinity of Panaca[25] and Pioche[26] [Nevada] planting some crops and exploring

---

service!" Lowell M. Durham, "The Role and History of Music in the Mormon Church," (M.A. Thesis, Iowa State University, July 1942) 29-30.

[23] Homes were built inside a fort, to protect against Indian attacks. According to James J. Adams, "The Fort was fifty six rods square, divided into ninety-two lots, each two rods wide and four rods deep. A street four rods wide separated the lots from the public corral, which was in the center and occupied ten acres of ground . . . . In the southeast corner of the Fort, a four rod square was reserved for building a log council house . . . . The wall when completed was twelve feet high, seven feet thick at the base, and three feet at the top. The water was brought under the wall at the northeast corner through a rock culvert and a flume and ran west, then northwest and on out through another culver to the fields. Each family had room for a garden and some fruit trees back of their house. Some very fine orchards and gardens were in the Public Square even down to the late nineties." Luella Adams Dalton, comp., *History of Iron County Mission: Parowan, Utah* (Utah: privately published, ca. 1970), 33-34.

[24] Located in east central California just north of Death Valley, and on the western edge of the Great Basin, the White Mountains rise to a respectable altitude of 14,246 feet.

[25] "The quaint town of Panaca was the first permanent settlement in southeastern Nevada and today remains largely unchanged from its early roots as a Mormon farming community. In fact, many of Panaca's residents can directly trace their ancestry to the town's original settlers. The small community was originally part of

that wilderness returning home when the army came peaceably into the valley of the Great Salt Lake.[27]

---

Utah, but congressional boundary reclassifications in 1866 moved the town into Nevada." See "Panaca, Nevada," www.panaca.travelnevada.com (accessed June. 3, 2009).

[26] Pioche is the county seat of Lincoln County. "Between 1540 and 1775, the Spaniards explored through the southwest region. Then in 1863 a local Indian revealed a good specimen of silver ore to 'Famous Scout, Prospector, Expert Rifleman, and Missionary to the Indians,' William Hamblin . . . who was said to be the first white man to settle in Meadow Valley. On Hamblin's first visit to the deposits in 1863, he managed to take samples and make several locations. He then transferred his samples to Salt Lake City; the result would be several expeditions to the region, which established the Meadow Valley Mining District." The town was named later after Francois L.A. Pioche, a San Francisco financier, who purchased the mining property. See "Lincoln County Historic Overview," Pioche Chamber of Commerce, www.piochenevada.com/history.htm (accessed June 3, 2009).

[27] "The Utah War, 1857-1858, was a costly, disruptive and unnecessary confrontation between the Mormon people in Utah Territory and the government and army of the United States. It resulted from misunderstandings that transformed a simple decision to give Utah Territory a new governor . . . . Had there been transcontinental telegraphic communications at the time, what has been referred to as "Buchanan's Blunder" almost certainly would not have occurred . . . . President James Buchanan moved quickly after his inauguration to find a non-Mormon governor for Utah. Then, apparently influenced by reports from Judge W.W. Drummond and other former territorial officials, he and his cabinet decided that the Mormons would resist the replacement of Governor Brigham Young. So, without investigation, the contract for mail service to Utah was canceled and 2,500-man military force was ordered to accompany Alfred Cumming to Great Salt Lake City. In the absence of formal notification of administration intentions, Young and other Mormon leaders interpreted the army's coming as religious persecution and adopted a defensive posture. Under his authority as governor, Young declared martial law and deployed the local militia, the Nauvoo Legion, to delay the troops. Harassing actions included burning three supply trains and driving hundreds of government cattle to the Great Salt Lake Valley. The 'scorched earth' tactics forced Albert Sidney Johnston's Utah Expedition [otherwise known as Johnston's Army] and the accompanying civil officials to improvise winter quarters (at Camp Scott and Eckelsville), near burned-out Fort Bridger, while the nation feared the worst. During

the winter both sides strengthened their forces. Congress, over almost unanimous Republican opposition, authorized two new volunteer regiments, and Buchanan, Secretary of War John B. Floyd, and Army Chief of Staff Winfield Scott assigned 3,000 additional regular troops to reinforce the Utah Expedition. Meanwhile, the Mormon communities were called upon to equip a thousand men for duty in the one hundred miles of mountains that separated Camp Scott and Great Salt Lake City. Despite his belligerent public posture, Brigham Young never intended to force a showdown with the U.S. Army. He and other leaders frequently spoke of putting homes to the torch and fleeing into the mountains rather than permitting their enemies to take over their property. Memories of earlier persecutions were invoked to build morale and prepare the people for possible further sacrifices. Early in 1858 exploring parties were sent to locate a place of refuge that Young believed to exist in the central Great Basin. By the time they returned with negative reports, the Utah War was over. That Young hoped for a diplomatic solution is clear from his early appeal to Thomas L. Kane, the influential Pennsylvanian who had for ten years been a friend of the Mormons. Communications and personal problems delayed Kane's approach to Buchanan, and not until after Christmas did he receive permission to go to Utah as an unofficial emissary. He reached Salt Lake City late in February, via Panama and California, and found the Mormon leadership ready for peace but doubtful about its feasibility. When the first reports of Kane's Camp Scott contacts with General Johnston were discouraging, Young's pessimism was confirmed. The 'Move South' resulted. On 23 March Young announced that the time had come to implement the 'Sebastopol' policy, a plan named after a strategic Russian retreat during the Crimean War. All the Mormon settlements in northern Utah must be abandoned and prepared for burning. Initially conceived as permanent, the evacuation began to be seen by the Mormon leadership as tactical and temporary as soon as word came that Kane was bringing Cumming to Salt Lake City without the army. Still, it was a relocation that dwarfed the earlier flights from Missouri and Illinois; approximately 30,000 people moved fifty miles or more to Provo and the other towns in central and southern Utah. There they remained in shared and improvised housing while the outcome of the Utah War was being determined. Kane and Cumming came to the Mormon capital in early April. Young immediately surrendered the gubernatorial title and soon established a comfortable working relationship with his successor. However, neither of the non-Mormons would encourage Young's hope that the army might be persuaded to go away, nor could they give him convincing assurance that Johnston's troops would come in peacefully. So the Move South continued. Meanwhile President Buchanan responded to rising criticism by publicly appointing two commissioners, Lazarus Powell and Ben McCulloch, to carry an amnesty proclamation to the Mormons. Upon reaching Utah in early June, they found Young and his colleagues willing to accept

In 1860 he married Mary Mitchell,[28] widow of William Mitchell, who was accidentally killed while logging in Parowan Canyon. From this union there was born one daughter, Mary Ann, his first child, his first wife being without children.[29]

In 1867 he married my mother, Caroline Mortensen,[30] a girl of Danish descent, she having come to Utah with her parents also in 1856

---

forgiveness for past offenses in exchange for accepting Cumming and the establishment of an army garrison in the territory. When Johnston's army marched through a deserted Salt Lake City on 26 June 1858 and then went on to build Camp Floyd forty miles to the southwest, the Utah War was over." Richard D. Poll, "The Utah War," *Utah History Encyclopedia*, ed. Allan Kent Powell (Salt Lake City: University of Utah Press, 1994). Thomas belonged, as did most of the adult, male population of the area, to the Utah Territorial Militia (Nauvoo Legion): 10th Regiment Battalion and served in the 1st Battalion, Parowan, also as Fifer. See Shirts, *A Trial Furnace*, 491.

[28] Thomas Durham's Journal states "April 5th 1860 – Married one of Bro. W.C. Mitchell's widows (Mary Moore Mitchell) with 4 children (3 boys & one girl). Bro. Amasa Lyman sealed her to me for time." See Thomas Durham Journal 1854-1871, ed. Paul D. Durham.

[29] Mary Ann Durham (b. Dec. 6, 1861, Paragonah, Iron, UT; d. Jan. 31, 1881; died Bluff, San Juan, UT; buried Bluff Cemetery, Bluff, UT. Spouse: Ole Hanson Bayles). See Utah Burials, Utah State History, http://history/utah.gov/apps/burials (accessed Dec. 5, 2008).

[30] Caroline Mortensen, born May 16, 1850, Haarbolle, Fanefjord, Praesto, Denmark, died August 19, 1915, Parowan, Iron, Utah, was the youngest of nine children born to Peder (by profession, a cooper—one who makes barrels or casks—and also a shoemaker) and Helena (Lena) Mortensen. She traveled at the age of six with her parents (ages 50 and 48) and six siblings: Anne Kirstene (called Stena) (24), Anders J. (22), Hans Jorgen (19), Lars (13), Mette Kirstene (variant spellings include Mettie Kerstina) (11), and Maria (or Mary) (9) from Copenhagen on the steamship *Rhoda*, along with 161 other emigrating Saints bound for Utah, under the leadership of Elder Johan A. Ahmanson, departing April 23, 1856, to Kiel (Germany), by Railroad to Hamburg, by steamer to Grimsby in England and then by railroad to Liverpool. They sailed from Liverpool on the ship *Thornton*. See Immigrant Ships Transcribers Guild: *Ship Thornton, From Liverpool, England to New York, June 15, 1856, District*

*of New York, Port of New York*, National Archives and Records Administration, Film M237, Reel 163, Transcribed by Sheila Jensen Tate, Mar. 31, 1999, See Immigrant Ships Transcribers Guild, "Ship Thornton," http://www.immigrantships .net/1800/ thornton 18560615_2.html (accessed Nov. 22, 2008). It lists the family as passengers numbering 463-471 in the "Lower Between Deck" and lists the children with the surname Peterson. (The children's surname was changed to Mortensen after immigrating.) It set sail on May 4, 1856, carrying an additional 600 Saints from Great Britain—764 total members of the church. It arrived in New York City on June 14, 1856. See Andrew Jensen, *History of the Scandinavian Mission*, 1927, 112. After arriving in New York, the emigrants had to travel 1,200 miles to Iowa City over 11 days. See Olsen, *The Price We Paid*, 7,11,12. She, along with her family, then crossed the plains with the James G. Willie Company, the fourth handcart company, which consisted of about 500 individuals, 100 handcarts and 5 wagons that departed Iowa City, Iowa July 15, 1856 and arrived in the Salt Lake Valley November 9, 1856 (just three weeks before the arrival of the Martin Company.) In spite of the heroic rescue, 68 of the company died. Caroline's daughter wrote that "despite her [Caroline's] tender age . . . she walked almost every step of the way across the plains, and often told us how very tired she was and how her poor feet ached. When they reached the Platte River, her brothers carried her across, for she was too small to have made it herself." See Isabella Durham McGregor, "The Life of Caroline Mortensen Durham, 1850-1915," February 1964, copy of typewritten manuscript, History Department, International Society Daughters of Utah Pioneers, Salt Lake City, 1. "One faithful Danish couple was Peder Mortensen, age 48, and his wife, Lena Mortensen, age 46, who were converted to the gospel in 1855. Due to a desire to gather to Zion and rejection by their community, they sold everything they owned in anticipation of their journey. They had land and animals. Together with their 8 children, ages 5 through 27, they traveled to Copenhagen, Denmark, to stay at the mission home until they could emigrate to Utah. The Mortensens' oldest son, Morten, was asked by the mission president to stay in Denmark and serve as a missionary. Morton, along with the rest of the Mortensen family, was concerned, but all agreed. The mission president promised the Mortensens that every one of them would reach Zion in safety because of Morten's willingness to stay and serve, along with the family's willingness to do without his much-needed help. Peder was physically disabled. He and his wife had planned to buy a wagon so that he could ride in it to the Salt Lake Valley. However, after hearing the counsel of their church leaders, they shared their money with other members of the company so that sufficient handcarts and supplies could be bought in Iowa City. Peder's disability kept him from walking. He rode in a supply wagon until about September 6, when the loads were adjusted due to a buffalo stampede. He had to be carried in a handcart from that point, until the company was rescued. Morten came to Utah after his three-in the handcart company just ahead of the one in which he came.[31] By this union[32] there were born ten children, five boys and five girls, all

---

year mission in 1858, two years after the rest of his family had all safely arrived in Zion." Paul D. Lyman, *The Willie Handcart Company* (Provo, Utah: BYU Studies, 2006), 62. The Mortensens said that "rawhide was taken from the carts and scraped and boiled and used as soup. Each day took its toll of strength and lives. One extremely cold day fourteen were buried in one grave. The Pedersen [Mortensen] boys helped dig the grave. (They were some of the few with the strength necessary) and the mother [and] Stene [Anna Kirstene] helped prepare the burial clothes which consisted of old and worn blankets. This was a sad day. The flour was doled out by the ounce and was guarded as a matter of life and death. One night father Peder had retired, putting his family's portion under his head. He awoke when he felt someone feeling to take it. He rose on his elbows and said, 'If you steal one morsel of food from the mouths of my hungry children, you shall not live to reach Zion.' The poor man did not; he froze to death that very night." "Mortensen Family History," MS 15877, photocopy of typescript, Church History Library, The Church of Jesus Christ of Latter-day Saints, Salt Lake City, 6-7. "After eight months of travel, the Mortensen family arrived in the Salt Lake Valley. They took a short rest, then were sent to Parowan to settle. President Young, upon learning of the services rendered by the family to help others be able to join the handcart company, personally arranged for teams and wagons to take the Mortensen family to Parowan. This trip took two weeks." See "Caroline Mortensen Durham, Women of Faith and Fortitude," eds. Ruby H. Morgan, Janet Durham Jackson and Dora Lee Durham Madsen, copy of typewritten manuscript, History Department, International Society Daughters of Utah Pioneers, Salt Lake City, April 18, 2000, 3.

[31] The James G. Willie Company, the fourth handcart company, which consisted of about 500 individuals, 100 handcarts and 5 wagons, departed Iowa City, Iowa July 15, 1856 and arrived in the Salt Lake Valley November 9, 1856 (just three weeks before the arrival of the Martin Company.) In spite of the heroic rescue, 68 of the company died. "The emigrants who made up Willie's company arrived at Iowa City on the 26th of June, and here met their first disappointment—the tents and handcarts, the one to afford them shelter, the other the means of conveying their food and bedding on the journey across the plains, were not, as yet provided; and in waiting for the manufacture of these necessary things the company was detained until the 15th of July. The journey through Iowa to 'Old Winter Quarters,' by this time known under the name of Florence, Nebraska, was accomplished in twenty-six days, since they arrived at Florence on the 11th of August and remained there until the 16th. The chief hardship of this stage of the journey was the midsummer heat, the dust; and

with the exception of one boy who died in infancy are alive today and active in church and civic affairs.[33]

---

when heavy rains converted this to mud, the heavy roads. The part of Iowa through which their route passed was then fairly well settled, and from the people of that state they received varied treatment. Sometimes they were met with good-natured badinage, at other times with threats of personal violence. At one point they were overtaken by a sheriff's posse with a search warrant issued by a justice of the peace, authorizing the posse to search to the very bottom of the few wagons for young women, alleged to be tied down in them with ropes. Of course the search revealed no such conditions as were alleged. At Des Moines an act of kindness varied the treatment. A Mr. Charles Good presented Captain Willie with 'fifteen pairs of children's boots.' There were some few desertions from the company in this first stage of the journey, eight in all who were persuaded to the step by inducements held out by the people of Iowa—'for the leeks and onions'—is Captain Willie's manner of phrasing it." Roberts, *A Comprehensive History of the Church of Jesus Christ of Latter-day Saints*, Century I, Vol. IV, 88.

[32] Their oldest daughter writes "Mother was the baby of the family. She was only seventeen when she decided to marry Father, whom she had met at choir practices where she sang soprano. Grandmother [Lena] Mortensen was very much opposed to the marriage, for she felt her baby girl was much too tender-hearted to go into polygamy and she dreaded to see her hurt. However, after the marriage she was pleased and happy and often said she couldn't have had a more wonderful son-in-law." Isabella Durham McGregor, "The Life of Caroline Mortensen Durham, 1850-1915," 8.

[33] The children from this union are as follows: Thomas Thompson Durham (b. Dec. 12, 1869, d. Dec. 25, 1946); John Durham, referred to above in the Journal as dying the day following his birth (b. Oct. 11, 1871, d. Oct. 12, 1871); Alfred Morton Durham (b. Sept. 23, 1872, d. Oct. 23, 1957); Lena Isabella Durham (b. Mar. 12, 1875, d. Sept. 18, 1969); Caroline Mamie Durham (b. Mar. 9, 1877, d. June 19, 1962); Sarah Anna Durham (b. June 6, 1879, d. Jan. 15, 1967); Mettie Eliza Durham (b. July 14, 1881, d. May 21, 1971); George Henry Durham (b. Sept. 12, 1883, d. Feb. 17, 1974); Alice Mary Durham (b. Feb. 8, 1885, d. Apr. 24, 1941); Wilford Mortensen Durham (b. July 1, 1890, d. Aug. 20, 1968). "When Wilford was born, something went very wrong, and Mother [Caroline] came close to leaving us. Once when she was terribly low, she saw Aunt Mary Morton [Thomas' first wife], who had died in Elsinore the year before, standing at the foot of her bed. It seemed to Mother there was a very thin veil between them, and Mother asked Aunt Mary to

Father made his livelihood from manual labor most of his life being engaged as foreman or manager of a carpenter shop which employed a number of men in the making of all kinds of furniture from native wood which was plentiful in the mountains near by. This concern which was known as the P.U.M.M.I., or Parowan United Manufacturing and Mercantile Institution, had a Co-op Store, a lumber mill, a shoe and harness shop, a tannery and this carpenter shop and supplied most of Southern Utah with the various products made and imported into this section. Father's skill as a wood turner made it possible for him to turn chair spindles, bed posts, and articles of this kind used in the making of various kinds of furnishings for the home. All the coffins used for burials were also made here according to measurement and besides making the coffins he furnished the music and was often the speaker at the funerals.[34]

---

take it away so she could see her more clearly. But 'Aunty' said no, she could not do that yet; it was not time for Mother to go. Mother was in her fortieth year when Wilford was born, and the remaining twenty-five years of her life were years of invalidism. She was bedfast for the first five years, after which she gained a little strength and was able to get from her bed into a rocking chair in which she spent most of her days. Although she was a poignant figure, she was never a pitiful one, but was always a joy to be around." Isabella Durham McGregor, "The Life of Caroline Mortensen Durham, 1850-1915," 8-9.

[34] "In England, Durham was a woodturning expert and he is known for making fine furniture. Durham and James Connell had their cabinet shop in the basement of the cotton factory. They were stalwarts in the Parowan United Mercantile and Manufacturing Institution (PUMI) organized in 1869. The cabinet shop acquired a reputation for quality and craftsmanship and supplied southern Utahns with furniture for many years. Items produced included double lounges, known as Mormon couches, and a pioneer 'hide-a-bed." See Connie Morningstar, *Early Utah Furniture* (Logan: Utah State University Press, 1976); and Marilyn Conover Barker, *The Legacy of Mormon Furniture* (Salt Lake City: Gibbs Smith Publisher, 1996), 95-97 as cited in Janet Burton Seegmiller, *A History of Iron County: Community Above Self* (Salt Lake City: Utah State Historical Society [and] Iron County Commission, 1988), 182. "The formal cooperative movement began in the late 1860s, led by the Mormon church's 'School of the Prophets.' Men over the age of sixteen met in these

He was either chairman or a member of the committee that sponsored and conducted the county fairs each autumn in the town, and these occasions brought people from all over the southern counties to witness the fine displays of fruits, grains and vegetables, and every form of handicraft that skilled workmen could make. These affairs usually lasted for three days and were interspersed with sports of various kinds, dances, musicals, etc.

Scarcely a week passed but what one or more people traveling through the state, stayed at our home. The family was friend makers and splendid entertainers. There always seemed to be room to make two or three extra beds and to provide good wholesome meals for the

---

'schools,' which were somewhat like modern-day chambers of commerce. The formation of Zion's Cooperative Mercantile Institution (ZCMI) ensued in 1868. Cedar City and Parowan established the Cedar Cooperative Mercantile Company and the Parowan Mercantile and Manufacturing Institution (PUMI) in 1869." Seegmiller, *A History of Iron County*, 78-79. According to the P.U.M.I. Minute Book, "Thomas Durham and James Connell were the master workmen who spent the rest of their lives managing the old P.U.M.I. Cabinet Shop. Many of the pioneer boys worked here as apprentices to learn the trade. Walter C. Mitchell started in at eight cents an hour, Albert Matheson started with five to seven and a half cents an hour. Thomas . . . and James . . . fashioned all kinds of furniture out of the native lumber; beds chairs, all kinds, congress chairs, rockers, big and little, dining room chairs, chests, old fashioned lounges that were a couch by day and a full-sized bed at night, tables, work tables, center tables, stands cupboards, desks with all kinds of pigeon holes, drawers and files to be shut up when not in use. Everything that went into the pioneer home as furniture was made here and last but not least coffins for their dead. The P.U.M.I. Cabinet Shop supplied the whole of Southern Utah with furniture for many years." Dalton, *Iron County Mission,* 364. "Early in Iron Mission years, George A. Smith had built a sawmill in Parowan, to which Samuel Gould added a pair of stones for grinding flour. The trades continued to flourish in Parowan with the addition of a tannery, Calvin Pendleton's gun and machine shop, William Holyoak's saddle and harness shop, Lorenzo Barton's wheelwright shop, Herman Bayle's carpenter shop, Morgan Richards' lime kiln, Thomas Davenport's pottery factory, Thomas Durham's cabinet mill and Peter Mortensen's tub and bucket factory." See Shirts, *A Trial Furnace*, 400.

many friends and acquaintances that so often called. It was because of this faculty and willingness to entertain, and perhaps because the family always set a good table, that so many of the general authorities of the church used to make our home their home when attending quarterly conferences, father realizing what a wonderful opportunity it gave his family to come in close contact with these fine men; and nearly every one of them at some time or another were entertained in our unpretentious home.[35]

His home life was an exceptionally happy one. The families were united, living under the same roof, and agreeing almost perfectly, the other members of the family taking as much interest in my mother's children as though we were their very own. This came about as a result of father's impartiality and the tact he used in ministering family

---

[35] Thomas and Caroline's daughter wrote that "Each Conference time our home would be filled with visitors, and we children would sleep on the floor so the visitors could have our comfortable beds. The General Authorities who came through our way usually stayed a day or two, or at least overnight, and Father always remarked what a privilege it was to have such fine people in his home, and Mother was equally pleased. The brethren must have enjoyed being with Mother and Father, for they always asked to stay at our home, and were graciously and warmly welcomed. President Heber J. Grant was a special friend of Mother's. When he was sent to Japan on a mission, he had some lovely pictures mailed to her, which were still at the home the last time I saw them. He also sent her books he loved. President Wilford Woodruff stayed with Father and Mother; also John Taylor, George Q. Cannon, and many, many others I can't recall. The last time [Apostle Abraham] Owen Woodruff and his wife were in Parowan . . . they were guests at our home several days. After bidding the family goodbye and getting into their white-topped buggy, Brother Woodruff came back to the house and asked Mother if he might always stay at our home when in Parowan. She warmly assured him that he could, that she would be happy to have him. He and his wife were on their way to Old Mexico. Sometime later we received word they had both contracted smallpox and died." Isabella Durham McGregor, "The Life of Caroline Mortensen Durham, 1850-1915," 8.

affairs, governing in the spirit of love and having companions who worked in perfect harmony with him in the home.[36]

---

[36] Lena Isabella reminisced about their home life by saying that "Mother [Caroline] and Aunt Mary Morton, or 'Aunty,' as we called her, lived under the same roof, but each had a separate apartment. However, we all ate together. We loved 'Aunty,' and I'm sure she returned our love for she treated us as though we belonged to her, too." "Mary Moore Mitchell lived in a separate home about two blocks north of the old Courthouse on the east side of Main Street. I often visited her and had many meals at her home. We thought highly of all her children—the three boys and one girl who were Mitchells—and loved Mary Ann. Mary Ann adored Father and was with him whenever possible. She married Hanson Bayles and shortly afterwards moved to San Juan They were with the original company who went through the "Hole in the Rock." See Isabella Durham McGregor, "The Life of Caroline Mortensen Durham, 1850-1915," 5. Actually Hanson Bayles was with the original exploring expedition of 1879 and the original company who went through the 'Hole-in-the-Rock' to colonize the San Juan region; Mary Ann didn't accompany Hansen until 1880. ". . . There is no better example of the indomitable pioneer spirit than that of the Hole-in-the-Rock expedition of the San Juan Mission. No pioneer company ever built a wagon road through wilder, rougher, more inhospitable country, still one of the least-known regions in America. None ever demonstrated more courage, faith, and devotion to a cause than this group of approximately two hundred fifty men, women, and children with some eighty wagons and hundreds of loose cattle and horses who cut a wagon passage through two hundred miles of this country. Even the wily mountain sheep could not have negotiated the Hole-in-the-Rock before it was given a 'face lifting' by these pioneer road builders. Today their feat seems well-nigh impossible." David E. Miller, *Hole-In-The-Rock* (Salt Lake City: University of Utah Press, 1966), ix, 143. Mary Ann Durham "became the wife of Hanson Bayles Nov. 3, 1880. Accompanying her husband to the San Juan country in 1880 she became a veritable pioneer of that place and took part in all the hardships incident to building up a new settlement in a desert. She died in childbed, Jan. 31, 1888, leaving her husband four small children, namely, Mary Ann, Hanson D., Emma Juliet and Caroline Elizabeth." Andrew Jensen, *LDS Biographical Encyclopedia*, Vol. 3 (Salt Lake City: Andrew Jensen History Company, 1920), 15. "On Nov. 9, he [Hansen] started with his young wife for the San Juan Mission, reaching Bluff Dec 22, 1880." Jensen, *LDS Biographical Encyclopedia*, 14. Lena Isabella continues to write that "they were difficult times in those years. It seemed to us she was at the ends of the earth, and the rare occasions when she came back to Parowan were times of great rejoicing. I remember once when word came that Mary Ann was coming. We children were in the potato patch helping to harvest the crop. Thomas came running

He was honored with numerous ecclesiastical positions, being a presiding elder of the branch in England; and was ordained to the office of Seventy in the 69th quorum shortly after arriving here, serving as a member and as one of the seven presidents of the quorum. He was later ordained to the office of High Priest and called into the High Council, in which office he served for some thirty-five years. He was President also of the Stake High Priests' quorum and was ordained to the office of Patriarch under the hands of the late Apostle, Abraham Owen Woodruff.[37] As a proof of his prophetic gift as a Patriarch, in blessing me before I had any sons, he said; "Your sons shall go to lands which are now in darkness and preach the gospel of the Lord, Jesus Christ." My one son, Eugene,[38] filled a mission to South America and Julian[39] is now in South Africa, and neither of these countries was open to missionary service when the blessing was given.

---

with the news, and we raced for home to get cleaned up. Since her husband could not be at home, she stayed all winter, and it was a delightful time for the family." See Isabella Durham McGregor, "The Life of Caroline Mortensen Durham," 5-6.

[37] Abraham O. Woodruff, born Nov. 23, 1872, Salt Lake City, Utah, son of President Wilford Woodruff. Member of the Quorum of Twelve Apostles from 1896 (age 23) until his death in 1904 (age 31). He died in El Paso, Texas, after contracting small pox while caring for his wife, who died from the disease two weeks previously. Another note about his church devotion worth mentioning would be Thomas' selection as one of the eleven directors of the United Order of Parowan in 1875. The United Order, under the direction of Brigham Young, lasted in Parowan from 1873 to 1876 and on the whole was not successful. Many were re-baptized into the order, and most of the leading families of the community participated in a common fund, but as with other southern Utah communities, it fell short of expectations. See Luella Dalton, *Iron County Mission*, 331-334.

[38] Eugene Richards Durham, b. Apr. 9, 1906; d. July 13, 1969

[39] Julian Richards Durham, b. May 25, 1912; d. May 24, 1992.

He dearly loved music and gave unstintingly of his time and talents in furthering this cause in the church.[40] As stated above he took charge of the music in the Parowan Ward two days after his arrival and with the exception of a short period while he was away on the "Underground,"[41] he so continued until his death. Besides the choir work, he organized the [The Parowan] Harmonic Society, an organization which produced high class secular music in the form of concerts and programs for various occasions and which developed a love for the better in music which has its influence in that section of the country to the present time.[42] On two occasions he was invited by

---

[40] His hymn, "Stars of Morning, Shout for Joy," was included in the hymnal for the church. *Hymns*, (Salt Lake City: The Deseret News Press, 1948), no. 164. It had been published previously in an earlier hymnal. See "Stars of Morning, Shout for Joy," *Deseret Sunday School Songs* (Salt Lake City, The Deseret News Press, 1909), no. 1. See Addendum 12.

[41] See Footnotes 49- 50 below for a discussion on the "Underground" and living in exile.

[42] To have established such a prominent, permanent musical organization "in Rocky Mountain country which had seen permanent settlers less than seventeen years was exceptional—a small rural community boasting its own choral society of approximately sixty voices, plus a brass band and a string orchestra. Communications were slow and uncertain in those early days. Instruments were scarce and expensive. Yet these early Mormon communities with scarcely an exception boasted similar accomplishments. On September 13, 1865, President [Brigham] Young and a group of high Church officials held two meetings at Parowan. [These were held at the Parowan Meetinghouse or Rock Church, built ca. 1862 and added to the National Register of Historic Places in 1976, No. 76001818. The Parowan Rock Church is the only edifice of Parowan preserved and restored from this early period.] There was 'singing by the Parowan Harmonic Society, who occupied a well-put-up stand on the west side of the bowery. Their singing is a credit to their leader [Thomas Durham]. . . .'" See Lowell M. Durham, "General Sherman and the Parowan Choir—A Little-known Story of Music on the Mormon Frontier," *Improvement Era*, 1943, 79, 122. "Here Brother Durham's choir, famed throughout the state, entertained us with fine singing, the women on the east and men on the

west. One night a big mass meeting was called to see what was the best way to light the church. Someone suggested buying a beautiful chandelier to hold the coal oil lamps. One of the brethren rose to his feet and said, 'What's the use buying a thing like that when no one but Brother Durham can play it?' But the chandelier was bought, and what a thrill it was to see it all lit up." Dalton, *Iron County Mission*, 325. According to James J. Adams, "There was always music, [on Pioneer Day] by the Martial Band, led by Capt. Thomas Durham, even as early as 1854—Parowan City spent $325.00 for brass band instruments." Dalton, *Iron County Mission*, 271. "The inhabitants of Parowan were again treated to a Vocal and Instrument Concert by the Harmonic Society of this place. The opening glee, 'Whom shall we let in,' was well sung, and the Chorus was swell'd by over sixty voices; after which followed that beautiful song, 'Evangaline,' which was delivered with much pathos. 'Just before the battle Mother,' and 'That dear old flat,' were well received; and the glees 'Happy Dreams,' and 'Memory Bells,' were appreciated and applauded. The Orchestral Band executed a well arranged and sublime composition of Professor Durham's: after which, 'The Old Arm Chair,' was beautifully sung by Mrs. Morris [Sarah Durham Morris]. Some 22 pieces (Glees and Songs,) were rendered during the two evenings, and the Society is rapidly progressing under the management and tuition of Professor T. Durham, who is laboring with much assiduity, in the advancement of Music." Josiah Rogerson to Editor, *Deseret News*, April 12, 1865. "Through the kindness of Bro. Geo. A. Smith, we have, from a letter to him, particulars of a Harmonic Society at Parowan, organized Nov. 1st, 1864, and consisting of 40 male and 24 females members. The Society gave a concert on the 2nd inst., when a variety of singing, comic and sentimental, solo, glee, trio, quartette, etc., was executed in a creditable manner, the choruses being sustained by upwards of fifty voices." "Parowan Harmonic Society," *Deseret News*, Aug. 23, 1865. "'I Have no Mother Now,' by Mrs. M.A. Durham [this is probably Thomas' wife, Mary Morton Durham] and Miss M.A. Morris [this is likely Thomas' sister, Sarah Durham Morris], received much admiration. Prof. Durham, accompanied by the Cabinet Organ, sang 'Many Changes I Have Seen,' after which, the Society rendered, 'When Johnny Comes Marching Home,' in good style; and that comic composition, 'The Song of all Songs,' brought much applause. Taking into consideration the Society's lack of musical stationery, and the difficulty of obtaining the same, it can be said they have made much progress and are now doing well, and with the valuable addition of the Cabinet Organ and its efficient organist, Prof. Durham, the Society have added, and will add, much to the advancement of the science of music and to the life of our town." Josiah Rogerson, Correspondence, *Deseret News*, Dec. 28, 1865. For additional references to the Parowan Harmonic Society, see also *Deseret News*, Dec., 7, 1864; Feb. 22, 1865; Feb. 24, 1865; Sept. 27, 1865.

President Brigham Young to bring his choir to Salt Lake City to sing at the General Conference of the church, the company traveling in wagons the 250 miles distance to so participate.[43] It was on one of these occasions in 1870 that this choir had the opportunity of singing for General William T. Sherman[44] who was traveling through the territory at the time.

General Sherman was weary and while bands were serenading and people were calling for him to come out and make a speech, nothing seemed to move him until this small choir went close to his hotel room and feelingly sang "Hard Times" and the General came out and made a talk to the choir and made the promise that as far as his influence might go, our people should never experience hard times again.[45]

---

[43] "The choir left on one of their trips to conference on the morning of September 25, 1870, when seventeen wagons left Parowan en route to Salt Lake City. It was a regular caravan of singers, who were like one big happy family as they jolted along over the rough, rocky road, singing songs and telling stories of their journey across the plains and from foreign lands across the ocean in sailing vessels. Then at night they would sing and dance around the campfire while someone played the violin. Arrangements had been made for the company to make camp in the Tithing Office yard and for their cattle to be cared for on the church farm. Food, such as bread, butter, vegetables, and fruit, was brought to the Tithing Office for the choir members. The Parowan choir led by Thomas Durham sang on Thursday, Friday, and Saturday. On Sunday, George Careless led the Tabernacle Choir with the Parowan choir assisting." Lou Jean S. Wiggins, comp., "History of Iron County," *Pioneer Pathways* (Salt Lake City: International Society Daughters of Utah Pioneers, Talon Printing, 2002), 5:71-72.

[44] William Tecumseh Sherman, (1820-1891) General in the Union Army during the American Civil War (1861-65) known for his military strategy and "scorched earth" policy used against the Confederate States. When Ulysses S. Grant became President, Sherman succeeded him as Commanding General of the Army (1869-83) and was responsible for the conduct of the Indian Wars in the western United States.

[45] "As early as 1864 we discover in our perusal of the records the first tangible results of his work in Parowan, when, in November of that year, he was instrumental in organizing 'The Parowan Harmonic Society, for the cultivation of sacred and

secular music.' (*Deseret News*, Nov. 21, 1864) A memorable high light of the Harmonic Society was reached five years later—a thrilling event never to be forgotten by any member of that group of music lovers. It was at 'October Conference' time in 1870. At this particular conference, the merits of the Parowan Harmonic Society had been recognized, and they had been invited by Brigham Young to journey to Salt Lake to furnish the musical selections for the meetings—an honor for which the various ward choirs vied constantly. The group set out in a covered wagon caravan nearly three weeks before the conference was scheduled to take place. The two hundred and fifty mile journey was a real undertaking in those days, the caravan averaging about twenty miles per day. It so happened that when they arrived in Salt Lake City that the Chief Commander of the United States Army was spending a few days in that city. Whitney, in his *History of Utah*, tells how the eminent solider, accompanied by his daughter, General Schofield, and other military officers, registered at the Townsend House, present site of the Hotel Utah, [It was actually located at the corner of West Temple and First South streets. It was the Continental Hotel and renamed in 1877.] and during their stay had a very sociable interview with President Young and other church leaders at the President's office. One evening, while Sherman was still in Salt Lake City, the townspeople gathered outside his hotel, clamoring for a view of their idol. The war-torn veteran had been serenaded the same evening by the Camp Douglas Band, but in spite of all this he had declined to put in an appearance and address the throng. 'An hour later, after the throng had dispersed to a small degree, the members of the Parowan choir, who were in Salt Lake to attend the conference, made their appearance and sang two or three pieces, which were followed by cries of 'Sherman,' 'speech.' This was followed by a call for 'Hard Times, come again no more,' which was very effectively rendered by the choir. General Sherman then made his appearance, and in a few well-chosen words acknowledged the compliment paid him by the singers.' The clamoring and pleading of the throng, plus the serenading of one of Uncle Sam's military bands had failed to impress the General. What they had failed to do, the Parowan Mormon choir had been able to accomplish with their sweet, sincere singing. That the hero of the March to the Sea was deeply touched is evident by his words to the choir: 'I address myself not to the crowd, but to this little band of singers, who, I understood, have traveled by team and wagon two hundred fifty miles to sing at their church conference. So far as it is in my power, I promise them 'that hard times shall come again no more' to this people.' He stated further that he did not intend to make a speech. He had heard the singers were from Parowan; he did not know Parowan, only by seeing it on a map." (*Journal History of the Church of Jesus Christ of Latter-day Saints*, Oct 4, 1870, Church History Library, Salt Lake City) As cited in Lowell M. Durham, "The Role and History of Music in the Mormon Church," (M.A. Thesis, Iowa State University, July 1942) 33-36. The *Deseret News* report is actually dated

Going to and from conference the choir entertained the people in many of the towns where they might chance to stay overnight.

He and his choir also furnished the music for the dedicatory services of the St. George temple in April 1877.[46] He organized and maintained a brass band also for many years and an orchestra that played for all the town dances and traveling shows which came to the town.

He composed quite a considerable share of the music he used in all of these various organizations and did practically all of the arranging of the music he used, writing it out by hand and suiting it to the purpose as occasion required. He kept constantly in touch with the new music material which was published and made use of it in many ways,

---

October 12, 1870: "Finding that 'no speech' was the order of the evening, the crowd gradually dispersed, until, at ten o'clock, not over a hundred or a hundred and fifty remained [from four to five hundred previously]. At this time the members of the Parowan choir, who are in to attend Conference, made their appearance and sang two or three pieces, which were followed by cries of 'Sherman,' 'speech.' The General was on the balcony, and in answer to these calls said 'No, no, I would rather hear the girls sing.' This was followed by a call for 'Hard Times, come again no more,' which was very effectively rendered by the choir . . . . He was gratified to behold the beautiful homes which the people while facing difficulties and trials of the severest kind, had built up in the desert, and his sincere wish was that they might live to enjoy them, and that to them 'Hard times would come again no more.'" See "The Serenade Last Night," *Deseret News*, October 12, 1898. See also J. Spencer Cornwall, *Stories of our Mormon Hymns* (Salt Lake City: Deseret Book, 1963), 181-183. Cornwall appears to be extracting without reference this thesis or another Lowell M. Durham article in the *Improvement Era*, which formed a chapter in Durham's M.A. thesis for Iowa State University. See Lowell M. Durham, "General Sherman and the Parowan Choir—A Little-known Story of Music on the Mormon Frontier," *Improvement Era*, 1943, 78, 122, 124-125.

[46] The St. George Temple was dedicated 6-8 April 1877, the first temple built and completed after the migration of the Latter-day Saints to the Utah Territory.

assisting all of the organizations with their programs, spending countless hours of his time in this service.[47]

His hobby was gardening; a lover of flowers and vegetables, and he never failed to have an abundance of both and his gardens were a thing of beauty for neatness and variety. He was in constant communication with the U. S. Department of Agriculture and tried out new varieties as they were developed and sent out by the department.

He also was voluntary weather observer for a number of years and was in charge of the experiment farm located in the valley under the direction of the U. S. experiment station at Logan, Utah.

He lived at Elsinore, Utah,[48] under an assumed name during the polygamy raid and during this episode had a number of exciting

---

[47] His many music interests kept him busy, which was attested by many. "A great little town is Parowan—one of the oldest in the south. The valley in which it lies raises thousands of bushels of grain, and any amount of fruit. But her famous product undoubtedly is sweet singers. With the possible exception of Beaver, a much larger place, Parowan, can boast of the best choir in the south, which is saying a great deal. To Thomas Durham belongs the credit for the high standard it has attained. He has wielded the baton in his little circle for forty years and will continue to do so if appearances count for aught, for twenty years more." "Prest. Snow at Nephi," *The Salt Lake Herald*, May 27, 1899, 1. "The most devout patriot would have been delighted with our celebration here yesterday of Washington's birthday. The Tabernacle, which will seat a thousand people, was crowded to excess. Many thought it the best celebration we had ever seen in this place, but while the present is more or less clear to us, the past is often a little dim. Our excellent choir, under the leadership of Prof. Thomas Durham, which is the main feature in all our celebrations, sang sweetly and with spirit the song Guard the Flag, and another fine patriotic song . . . . Prof. Durham's orchestra played a fine selection." Wm. C. M'Gregor, Letter to Editor, *Deseret Evening News*, March 2, 1898, 5. "Monday evening at 8 o'clock a grand sacred concert was given by the choir, under the direction of Professor Thomas Durham. Selections were rendered from the oratorios of St. Paul and Elijah; also some choice quartettes, solos, etc. The choir was assisted by Professor A. M. Durham as accompanist. He also gave some very fine selections on the piano and three very choice tenor solos, which were very much appreciated." "Conference at Parowan," *The Salt Lake Herald*, Sept. 22, 1900, 5.

experiences.[49] His first wife died also at this time and he returned to
Parowan and resumed his former activities, having not been arrested,
but having lived in exile, for conscience sake for some four years.[50] He

---

[48] Elsinore was first settled in the spring of 1874 by James C. Jensen, Jens Iver
Jensen, and others. The town was given its official name at the suggestion of
Mormon Stake President Joseph A. Young because the site reminded him of
Elsinore, Denmark, where he had visited. The town had an earlier name of Little
Denmark because many of the early settlers were immigrants of that country.
Elsinore is in Sevier County and is located on US-Highway 89 and is six miles south
of Richfield.

[49] He used the name Thomas Thomson during the four years he spent at Elsinore.
"Thomas Thomson from nowhere came to Elsinore some 20 years ago. He built a
fine choir and good brass band and was the leading spirit in the musical world for
several years. That same personality now dumps into Elsinore in the form of Thomas
Durham from Parowan last Monday. It was whispered from man to man 'we are
going to have a reception for Thomas (Thomson) Durham tonight in the Relief Hall.'
We did have a reception—one of the grandest affairs we ever had. The victim was
placed in a big rocker and a fine program of vocal and instrumental music was
carried out. Thomas Durham furnished a couple of numbers. One extreme curiosity
of the evening was on a suggestion of Bishop J. I. Jensen. Thomas Durham gathered
his old choir, of which seven members were present and sang the hymn, 'Oh, My
Father,' to the tune composed by Mr. Durham many years ago. The seven choir
members were Eliza Sylvester, Minnie Frandsen, Stene B. Hansen, J.I. Jensen and
H.P. Hansen." "Elsinore,"    *Reaper*, Sept. 12, 1907. See also *Richfield Reaper*,
March 11, 1909.

[50] The editor of this annotation wants to make clear that Thomas was at this time
married to Mary Morton, Mary Moore Mitchell and Caroline Mortensen at the same
time. Thomas' daughter writes that "When Father was on the 'underground' during
the trying days of polygamy, he moved to Elsinore and lived there for several years
with Aunt Mary [Morton]. She was lonely without children, and asked Mother
[Caroline Mortensen] if she could 'borrow' some of us; so we took turns—Thomas,
Alfred, and I—in staying in Elsinore with her and Father." See Isabella Durham
McGregor, "The Life of Caroline Mortensen Durham, 1850-1915," 5. His first wife
(Mary Morton) "died also at this time" (during the period of the polygamy raids and
exile which lasted "four some years.") Thomas, it may be noted, was legally, in the
eyes of the government, married to Mary Morton, and not to the other two.
Therefore, he could have enjoyed a modicum of safety living with her in Elsinore

was warned in dreams on more than one occasion of deputy marshal raids and thus prepared to avoid them when they came to try to make an arrest. He had charge of the music in the Elsinore ward during this sojourn and was just as active as he had been in his home town. He made many staunch friends in this locality and was especially indebted

---

and would have been subject to greater jeopardy in Parowan. Many members as well as leaders went into hiding in the 1880s—in the "underground" as it was called— either to avoid arrest or to avoid having to testify regarding their polygamous marriages. Mormon Church President John Taylor died while in hiding. "During President [John] Taylor's ministry, persecution of the Church grew in intensity. Three missionaries were killed in the southern states, and the U.S. secretary of state attempted to prevent Mormon immigrants from entering the United States, citing them as potential lawbreakers because of the Church's practice of polygamy. Congress passed the Edmunds Act of 1882, declaring polygamy to be a felony. Under its provisions, polygamists could not vote, hold public office, or serve on juries. The General Authorities discussed the Church's course of action as well as their hopes for achieving statehood. Wilford Woodruff later wrote that 'President Taylor with the rest of us came to the conclusion that we could not swap of[f] the Kingdom of God or any of its Laws or Principles for a state government' (*Wilford Woodruff Journal*, Nov. 27, 1882). Mounting antipolygamy prosecution, known as 'the Crusade,' led to the arrest and imprisonment of hundreds of men and women. President Taylor instructed polygamous Saints to establish places of refuge in Mexico and Canada, and he and his counselors withdrew from public view to live in the 'Underground.' During his last public sermon he remarked, 'I would like to obey and place myself in subjection to every law of man. What then? Am I to disobey the law of God? Has any man a right to control my conscience, or your conscience? . . . No man has a right to do it' (*JD* 26:152). Persecution intensified in 1887 with the passage of the Edmunds-Tucker Act, which abolished women's suffrage, forced wives to testify against their husbands, disincorporated the Church, and escheated much of its property to the United States. For two and a half years, President Taylor presided over the Church in exile. The strain took a great toll on his health. He died on July 25, 1887. . . while living in seclusion . . . in Kaysville, Utah." See Paul Thomas Smith, "John Taylor," *Encyclopedia of Mormonism*, ed. Daniel H. Ludlow (New York: Macmillan, 1992), 1440-1441.

to the Sylvester family[51] for so many kindnesses shown him while there.

Perhaps his greatest spiritual experiences[52] were in fulfillment of Elder Wheelock's prediction about receiving Heavenly music in his dreams. This manifestation came to him not only once but on several occasions, and true to the blessing, he wrote these numbers and sang them himself in two temples, the St. George and Manti, and since this time they have no doubt been heard in all of the other temples. One of these known as the *"Nephite Lamentation"* may be worthy of mention here. In his dream, father was in a strange country seemingly, somewhat wooded and near a river bank, and some rather strange looking people were on the bank, as he thought, taming a horse, by having it in the water and throwing a blanket over it as they held it by

---

[51] This may be in reference to Bishop Sylvester's family. "[In 1876] President A. K. Thurber selected Joshua William Sylvester as Bishop." See Jean S. Greenwood, comp., "History of Sevier County," *Pioneer Pathways* (Salt Lake City: International Society Daughters of Utah Pioneers, Talon Printing, 1999), 2:17.

[52] "Mother [Caroline] often accompanied Father [Thomas] on his journeys to Salt Lake for Conference, and she was with him on the occasion when the man (who [sic] they felt was one of the Three Nephites) and his family visited them on the road." Isabella Durham McGregor, "The Life of Caroline Mortensen Durham, 1850-1915," 11. Mettie Durham Robinson [Mickelson] relates that it was in the spring of 1880 when Thomas, Caroline, and son, Thomas Jr., were camped near the Provo River. It has been raining and the roads were muddy when a man approached on a beautiful black pony with four white feet and not a speck of dirt on them. After inquiring after his name, the man said that his wife and two sons would be coming along soon and would he not invite them to remain until he returned. He said that the roads were good on the way to Salt Lake City. He also reported about an accident in Springville involving a train and wagon team. Thomas wondered how he would have known about the accident, he coming from the other direction. The rest of the party arrived in a black surrey with all horses in black and outfitted with white feet. When about to leave, Thomas glanced back to get a last look at the beautiful team, but they had disappeared. See Dalton, *Iron County Mission*, 297-298.

a rope as it was made to swim up and down the stream. Presently a number of men of the same character gathered, when one of the number who seemed to be in charge of the group had them form in a semi-circle near the river. Having thus formed, the one in charge directed one of the men who had an old type brass instrument, to take his place in the center of the semi circle which he did, and on this instrument he played this melody. Father noticed a few more movements and then awakened. He immediately went to sleep again and the music was repeated, just as before, but without seeing anything in his dream. He awoke and arose from his bed, went, to the organ and played it by which means he was able to remember it and later write it out.[53]

---

[53] "I was standing alone at the head of a large river that was running west, on a narrow neck of land about 3 rods wide and 3 rods long sloping about 3 feet down to the water's edge. I stepped to one side looking west as the river ran. The country was heavily timbered. I was gazing down the river, expecting some of my folks to come—it was nearly sundown. Suddenly I heard a rustling in the timber behind me. I looked about me for I thought myself alone and I saw coming toward me what I thought was a Navajo Indian. I looked west again and saw a striped blanket floating on top of the water. Two men stepped down to the water's edge to lift the blanket up when a pony came from under it. By this time, the Indian that I first saw stepped down and put his hand on the Pony's neck and led him out of the water. I smiled and thought that a curious way to gentle a horse and he gave me a look as much as to say that it was none of my business. I looked around and saw about thirty Indians coming toward, me. When they got to where I was standing they formed a circle, the chief standing on the east side. He pointed his finger to a young man on the west who had a brass horn in his hand. This young Indian stepped out and went down to the water's edge and played a tune, the Nephite song of lamentation. After he finished, he came back to his place. The chief then motioned to another man to his left who had a gun in his hand. He went down to the same place and fired his gun into the air. Then I awoke. I remembered the tune and lay wondering whether to go to the organ and play it over and by that means I would not forget it; but I went to sleep again and I heard the same tune again but saw nothing. I woke up just as the tune was finishing. It was just breaking day and I got up and went to the organ and played the tune. Afterwards I wrote it and arranged it for the choir. This was in fulfillment of a blessing that Elder Cyrus H. Wheelock promised me in England in

1851. In that blessing he told me that angels would reveal to me in my sleep, music that is sung in the Heavens. I have also had five other pieces besides this one revealed to me in my sleep and we sing them in the choir. Some time after this, Bro. Wheelock and Patriarch D. Tyler of Beaver were staying at my house when Bro. Wheelock asked me to relate the above dream. This I did. He then asked me and my family to sing it to him to the tune [words] of "O My Father." [See Addendum No. 14.] After we had sung it, Bro. Tyler said he had the same vision that I saw. He said that those men that I saw were a remnant of the Nephites after a heavy battle with the Lamanites when thousands of them were slain and after the gun was fired that I heard in my dream, they sang a song of lamentation. Then the chief lectured them for their disobedience to the prophet Mormon. Bro, Tyler gave us this speech in the Nephite language and then in English and I can testify that he did it under the influence of the Holy Spirit as can all who were in the room. – Respectfully, (signed) Thomas Durham." See photocopy of typewritten statement attributed to Thomas Durham in possession of editor (n.p., n.d.). See also See Mamie Durham Orton and Sarah Durham Connell, "Two Hundred Fifty Miles to Conference in a Covered Wagon," ed. Luella Dalton, copy of typewritten manuscript, History Department, International Society Daughters of Utah Pioneers, Salt Lake City, April 18, 2000, 3. "In many settlements of southern Utah a striking melody is used to the hymn, 'O My Father, Thou That Dwellest,' etc. The origin of this tune is given as follows by Brother Thomas Durham of Parowan: In a dream, in the year 1880, I stood at the head of a large river which was running toward the west. A narrow strip of land, about two rods wide, projected down the river a distance of about two rods. I was looking, in my dream, for some of our people to come up the river, and while I was thus engaged I heard a rustling noise behind me in the underbrush, the country back of me to the east being heavily timbered. As I turned I saw a young, tall, slim-built Indian coming towards me. I turned around again facing the river and saw two of the brethren whom I knew who stepped down to the water's edge, where was floating an Indian blanket. These brethren stepped on the blanket and an Indian pony came from under it. By this time the young Indian had come, and he took the pony by the mane and led him out of the water. I smiled because I thought this was the way in which they tamed their ponies. As I was thus pondering he cast a rather severe look to wards me, as much as to say that it was none of my business what he was doing. When I looked again in the direction of the brethren who had stepped on the blanket they were gone, as was also the young Indian, and I was again left alone. I turned my eyes toward the east and was astonished to see about twenty-five or thirty good looking Indians coming in my direction. They passed onto the neck of the land near which I was standing, and formed a circle. The chief stood on the east side and beside him was a young fine-looking Indian with a brass horn in his hand. The chief pointed his finger at him and he stepped out to the west end of the land near the

Elder Wheelock was about this time, a regular caller at father's home. He was sent out by the authorities to gather means for the

---

water, where he played a tune, and then came back and took his place in the circle. Then the chief pointed to another Indian who had a rifle and he stepped to the same place and fired the rifle, the noise of which awakened me. For a short time I lay and wondered if I had not better arise and go to the organ and play the tune which I had heard. It had made such an impression on my mind that I felt confident I could do so, and was afraid that should I go to sleep I might forget it. While thus reflecting I fell asleep and heard the same tune again played but did not see anything or anybody. When I again awoke I arose, dressed myself, went the organ and played the tune. The act of playing over a tune always makes such an impression upon my mind that I never forget what I once play in this manner. I afterwards arranged the tune for the choir and it has been sung in many wards. The above incident is the fulfillment of a blessing given me under the hands of Elder C. H. Wheelock in England in the winter of 1851. He told me that heavenly messengers would reveal music to me in my sleep, and that I should write and sing the same to the Saints. I have seen this promise come to pass. I have five or six other tunes in addition to the one accompanying this article which I received in dreams. I afterwards wrote them out and we now sing them in our meetings. In the year 1884, Elders Daniel Tyler and C. H. Wheelock were visiting at my house. Brother Wheelock requested me to sing a verse of the dream tune, which I did. Brother Tyler then said he had seen all my dream and more, whereupon he commenced to speak in tongues in the Nephite language. He also gave the interpretation of my dream. He said the tune I had heard was a song of lamentation which the Nephites sung each evening at sundown, and after the tune was ended the chief would address the assembled throng and condemn them for their disobedience towards the Prophet Mormon. These events, as he informed me in his remarks occurred just previous to the extinction of the Nephite race from this continent. (Signed) Thomas Durham. It is not at all unreasonable to believe that many things concerning the ancient people who dwelt upon this continent will be revealed. Not only their written words, but their melodies may yet find happy acceptance among the Latter-day Saints. No doubt many of their productions were most excellent." See "A Remarkable Composition," *The Contributor*, Vol. 15, 1893-1894 (Salt Lake City, Deseret News Publishing Company, 1894). "'O My Father' . . . gained renown in Utah not only for its heavenly origins, but also for the graceful way it handled the text. The beginning of each line consists of a lilting three-note figure that suits either a long-short or short-short pair of syllables with relative ease." Michael Hicks, "'O My Father': The Musical Settings," *BYU Studies* 36, (1997).

erection of the Manti Temple and on these visits stayed at our home. He had called in a number of the local brethren to discuss the matter in hand, and. in the course of the conversation asked father if he had received any more music as promised in the blessing given in England. Father related this dream and played the music and at the request of Patriarch Daniel Tyler of Mormon Battalion fame,[54] he played it over again. Brother Tyler arose and began speaking, and among other things said that what father had seen was the very thing that happened immediately after the terrible slaughter of the Nephites by the Lamanites, when all but some three dozen men were left of that once mighty nation. He said that they were in the habit of meeting periodically and going through such a program, in lamentation for their loved ones and friends who had been slain. He further said that if father had seen a little further in his dream he would have heard the leader of the group make a talk. The gift of tongues then came on Brother Tyler and. he spoke for several minutes, giving, by imitation, the talk made by this leader, the substance of which, as interpreted was that had they listened to the words of Mormon and Moroni, this great calamity might have been averted.[55]

---

[54] Daniel Tyler (1816-1906) had been a member of Zion's Camp and attended the School of the Prophets. He filled several missions for the church, and was one of the men who responded to President Brigham Young's call to serve in the Mormon Battalion with the United States Army. Tyler is perhaps best known for his authorship of the book *The Mormon Battalion in the Mexican War*. He was ordained a High Priest Sept. 24, 1844 and a Patriarch Dec. 10, 1873 by Brigham Young. See Mormon Battalion Association, "Daniel Tyler," http://www.mormonbattalion.com/ history/members/tyler/index.html (accessed Dec. 8, 2008).

[55] "The melody of the "Nephite Lamentation" was given to Thomas Durham, of Parowan, Utah, in a dream. A promise had been made to Thomas Durham that he should be visited by heavenly beings. In fulfillment of the promise, a young man, who was said to be one of the twenty-four Nephites surviving the last great battle between the Nephites and Lamanites at the Hill Cumorah, came to his room and played this melody on a brass horn. Apparently for the purpose of impressing the

tune upon Brother Durham's memory, it was repeated three times. In its rendition it seems that the high note in the second strain of the melody was beyond the range of the instrument but by the expression on the face of the young Nephite it was apparent that he was trying to reach a higher note. Brother Durham, being a musician, readily replaced the missing note to complete the melody. The rendition so impressed him that he was awakened and immediately arose and wrote the music of the tune to preserve it." See "History of the 'Nephite Lamentation,'" *The Utah Genealogical and Historical Magazine*, July, 1922, 95. "The melody, having been preserved by Brother Durham after the dream, he later adapted it to the words of the favorite Mormon hymn, 'O My Father,' and frequently sang it in public." See *The Relief Society Magazine*, ed. Susa Young Gates, VI, No. 6, (June 1919), 369-370. See also Hector Lee, *The Three Nephites: The Substance and Significance of the Legend in Folklore* (Albuquerque, The University of New Mexico Press, Publications in Language and Literature, number 2, 1949), 113. One author writes that "when I was a boy, my father returned from a trip to southern Utah with a story about the hill Cumorah which impressed me very much. He had visited Thomas Durham who related a remarkable dream. I have since heard this dream told with considerable variation, but as far as this incident is concerned the important thing is my own recollection of the details as told by my father." He continues by explaining that he visited the Hill Cumorah with the intention of seeing the stream that Durham had seen in his dream. "To my surprise I was told there was no stream within some miles of Cumorah. That seemed strange to me. I have always believed in dreams, especially when there is reason to think they are inspired. And as a boy I had accepted this as a divine manifestation to Thomas Durham—a manifestation so impressive that Brother Durham, who was a musician, was unable to rest until he had arisen from his bed and written the melody. And now I was told no such stream existed . . . . My disappointment was soon overshadowed, in part at least, by the beauty and inspiration of the surroundings . . . . As we walked along the road, [toward the Smith farm and Sacred Grove] I looked back towards the hill and decided to take a picture . . . . To reach the spot . . . it was necessary to climb through a fence and enter a pasture. Then I discovered that my feet were wet and that the grass around me was of a variety which grows only when there is an abundance of water. The dream and the stream came back. In the meadow was unmistakable evidence that here was an old river bed. To the east then winding around the hill to the south and extending as far as the eye could see, the water course was clearly marked from where I stood. The direction was toward the numerous lakes that dot the country south of Manchester, the largest being Seneca Lake." See John D. Giles, "From the Green Mountains to the Rockies," *Improvement Era*, November 1929.

Father was one who keenly sensed appropriateness in the selection of music for the various occasions, whether for religious or secular affairs, making choice of those numbers which were strictly in keeping with the sermon or sermons delivered or the program at hand.

He had an abiding faith in the mission of the Prophet Joseph Smith, and gave a life of unselfish service in the interest of the restored gospel and the people among whom he labored.

He was kindly disposed, and had a keen sense of humor, read much, knew what was going on in the world and although well along in years never grew old in spirit, but enjoyed a good time as long as he lived.

He enjoyed good health up until a few days before he died and was up and dressed, an hour or two before the end came.

His death occurred on the 4th of March 1909,[56] in his 81st year and was laid away in honor by his family and many friends in the family plot in Parowan,[57] where so much of his life had been spent.

---

[56] "He had been ailing for some time which developed into an illness which caused his demise. Mr. Durham was rather a noted character in southern and central Utah history. He moved from England to Parowan in 1856 and except for four years, in which he resided in Elsinore, made that his permanent home. He was associated with musical work all his life. As a choir leader he was known extensively and has been characterized by no less a personage then Apostle Whitney as the best posted man in Utah on the Hymnology of the Latter-day saints. One of the things which made him famous was the 'dream music' which has become widely known for its setting to the famous Mormon hymn, 'O My Father,' and which has been sung extensively throughout Utah. This music was given to him in a dream about 25 years ago. He dreamt of hearing the music upon a brass horn in the hands of one of the Nephites of old. The dream was repeated three times and the last time he arose from his bed and committed the music to paper and later sent it to the Juvenile Instructor where it was published to the words mentioned. Eighteen years ago Mr. Durham moved to Elsinore and became the leader of the local choir and band of that town. "Death of Former Resident of Sevier," *Richfield Reaper*, March 11, 1909. "Prof. R. Maeser represented the faculty at the funeral services, held over the remains of Patriarch Thomas Durham at Parowan last Saturday." "Murdock Academy," *Beaver City Press*, March 12, 1909.

This paper prepared by Alfred M. Durham, third son of Thomas and Caroline Mortensen Durham, Salt Lake City, UT. Read in Camp 17 Oct 1936.

---

[57] Parowan City Cemetery, (300 South Highway 143, Parowan, UT 84761). Plot location: 06-16-06.

# THOMAS DURHAM JOURNAL 1854-1871[1]

## Edited by Paul Denis Durham

"Thomas Durham

Commenced

Writing This Journal

On The

5th of January – 1854

From Other Papers, Books, &c.

Up to that date"[2]

---

[1] Thomas Durham (1828-1909). The transcription of the original hand-written journal (19 pp. 6.5" x 7.5" book), was prepared under the direction of G. Homer Durham, grandson (b. Feb. 4, 1911, Parowan, Utah, d. Jan. 10, 1985), while President of Arizona State University, Tempe, Arizona, during 1963. (Thomas Durham, Thomas Durham Journal 1854-1871, MS 1456, photocopy of typescript, Church History Library, The Church of Jesus Christ of Latter-day Saints, Salt Lake City.) A later, annotated typescript, edited with modern spelling and punctuation by G. Homer Durham was prepared by Beth S. Rasmussen, on August 18, 1982, under the supervision of Elder Durham as Church Historian and Recorder (MS 7644). Many dates were blank in the original and were inserted by Elder Durham, Feb. 16, 1966. Both copies reside at the Church History Library, Salt Lake City, UT. The original journal is not housed at the Church History Library, and may still be in the possession of G. Homer Durham's family or descendents. This new transcript (2009) has been edited by Paul Denis Durham (great-grandson, b. 1949), grandson of Alfred Morton Durham (1872-1957), son of Alfred Richards Durham (1918-1983), with additional footnotes and clarifications. Spelling and punctuation, for the most part, remain true to the original (e.g., *&c* for etc.)

[2] See Addendum No. 17 for photocopy of original title page.

Thomas Durham[3] is the son of John and Isabella Durham who were born at Whitby in Yorkshire.[4] John was born on the 18th of Dec. 1790 and Isabella on the 20th of Jan 1800 and were married on the 18 of Feb. 1824. Remained there a short time then moved to Oldham in Lancashire[5] in order to better their circumstances which they did and

---

[3] Some records, including several descendent family group sheets, show the author's full name as Thomas Washington Durham, but no direct confirmation has been provided that he had a middle name..

[4] John Durham (b. Dec. 18, 1790, Whitby, Yorkshire, England, d. Jan. 10, 1863); Isabella Thompson (b. Jan. 20, 1800, Whitby, Yorkshire, England, d. Mar. 31, 1883). Whitby is an historic town in the Scarborough district of North Yorkshire on the northeast coast of England, facing the North Sea, which dates back to 657 A.D. It is situated 47 miles from York. In 1753 the first whaling ship set sail from Whitby to Greenland and began a new phase in the town's development. "It was here, at the Synod of Whitby in 664 AD, that the Saxon Christians decided to adopt the customs of the Roman Catholic Church instead of the Celtic Church. The council was held in Whitby Abbey, an important monastery founded by St. Hilda, a Saxon princess, in 657 AD. In the centuries that followed, Whitby hosted such notable figures as St. Caedmon (the first English poet), William Scoresby (a whaler featured in *Moby Dick*), Captain James Cook, and Bram Stoker (who set much of *Dracula* in Whitby)." Sacred Destinations, "Whitby." http://www.sacred-destinations.com/england/whitby.htm (accessed Nov. 20, 2008).

[5] Oldham was the center for an agricultural district with a woolen industry until the 19th century, when it became a major cotton-spinning and weaving town. "Although Oldham's existence can be traced back to the 11th century, it was the Industrial Revolution—and cotton in particular—that laid the foundations for the town's prosperity. By the end of the 19th century Oldham was recognized near and far as nothing less than the greatest cotton spinning town in the world." Oldham England, "Town of Oldham England," http://wwp.greenwichmeantime.com/time-zone/europe/uk/england/oldham/index.htm (accessed Oct. 25, 2008). It wasn't until the American Civil war and the blockade of cotton from the Confederate Southern States by the Union, that there was a significant decline of raw cotton to the mills of England that triggered the decline of the cotton industry (1861-1865) from which it never fully recovered. "The town, which is one of the most important seats of the cotton manufacture in the world, owes its prosperity in great part to its situation on

settled to make a home for themselves. On the 6th of June 1825 they had a daughter which they named Sarah.[6] And on the 2nd of May 1828 I, Thomas, their son was born at Oldham in Lancashire. And on the 22 of August 1831, John their son was born at Oldham.[7] And on the 3rd of

---

the edge of the Lancashire coal-field, where the mineral is very easily wrought . . . . The total number of persons engaged in the industry is over 30,000, the annual consumption of cotton being over 700,000 bales, or about one-fourth of the whole quantity of cotton imported into the United Kingdom . . . . The population . . . in 1801 had increased to 12,024, in 1841 to 42,595, in 1861 to 72,333 . . . . Although consisting chiefly of monotonous rows of workmen's houses, interspersed with numerous immense factories and workshops, Oldham has some good streets and a number of imposing public buildings." *The Encyclopedia Britannica*, 9th ed., (Philadelphia: J.M. Stoddart, 1884) s.v. "Oldham," 780-781.

[6] "Sarah joined the Church, emigrated to Utah, and was the wife of William Morris. I knew her as 'Aunt Sarah Morris' from my father's recollections." This annotation was added to the typewritten copy by G. Homer Durham. His additional footnotes have been added throughout this edited version. See Thomas Durham, Thomas Durham Journal 1854-1871, MS 7644, ed. G. Homer Durham, photocopy of typescript, Church History Library, The Church of Jesus Christ of Latter-day Saints, Salt Lake City, 1982, Footnote No. 1, 1. "In early life she joined the Church of Jesus Christ of Latter-day Saints, having been converted by Cyrus H. Wheelock. She studied music under Prof. W. Warrington along with her brother, Thomas Durham, and was closely associated with him in choral work the greater part of their lives. She led the choir in the branch [in England] where she resided after her brother emigrated to Utah. She was married to Wm. Morris August 20, 1848, and became the mother of nine children, five of whom survive her. In 1862 with her husband and children she emigrated to Utah, arriving in Parowan in October of that year, and resided here ever since, sharing the trials and hardships incident to settling new countries. One severe trial was the death of a 10 year old daughter who was buried by the wayside at Rocky Ridge, Wyoming, while she was en route to Utah. She was a member of the Parowan choir for many years, and went to Salt Lake City in 1870 when the choir had the privilege of singing to Gen. W. T. Sherman." "Aged Lady Dead," *Parowan Times* (July 5, 1916).

[7] "Birth dates inserted by G. Homer Durham, b.1911, a grandson of Thomas Durham, from a *Latter-day Saints Family Record; Containing the names, births, deaths, burials, &c, of the Families of the. . .* [Durhams and Thompsons]; Commencing . . . with [John Durham the first son of Sarah Durham, etc. . . . .] Published for the Manchester Conference, Nov.1852, by Jonathan Midgley, under

April 1834 Isabella their daughter was born at Oldham. And on the 1st of Sept. 1836 Mary Ann their daughter was born at Oldham. and on the 26th of June, 1841 Elisabeth their daughter (died June 24th 1841) was born[8] at Stalybridge,[9] Cheshire [County] where they removed to in March 1837 on account of the mills being turned out, and, the shoemakers were also on the strike for more wages. My father being a shoemaker by trade and my mother a boot and shoe binder; and, none of the children old enough to work. But shortly after coming to Stalybridge my sister Sarah began to work in the cotton mill and my father began to learn me to be a shoemaker but did not stay at it long because I did not like it very well. It did not agree with me so my mother got me some work in Jonathan Mills Bobbin Shop in the latter end of 1839[10] where I remained jobbing about until 1843. Then I went

---

the Pastoral charge of Cyrus H. Wheelock . . . when Samuel W. Richards was President of the British Isles." G. Homer Durham, in MS 7644, footnote 1a, 1. The children of John Durham and Isabella Thompson Durham were: Sarah Durham, b. June 6, 1825; Thomas Durham, b. May 2, 1828; John Durham, b. Aug. 22, 1831; Isabella Durham, b. April 3, 1834; Mary Ann Durham, b. Sept. 1, 1836; Elizabeth Durham, b. circa June 24, 1841.

[8] The date of Mary Ann's birth was omitted in the original. G. Homer Durham inserted the date of June 26, 1841, but this is obviously erroneous, since he inserts the date of June 24, 1841 as the death date.

[9] Stalybridge, county of Cheshire, is a small town in the north-west of England lying at the foothills of the Pennines, which are also known as the backbone of Britain, 8 miles east of Manchester. In 1831 the population was 14,216 and inhabited houses numbered 2,357. The town of Stalybridge was the creation of the Industrial Revolution. Cotton and the spinning industry lead to the development of Stalybridge as a town. The name Stalybridge originally came about due to the local Manor of Stayley, and the bridge which crossed the River Tame. (Not to be confused with the River Thames.) A song written by Jack Judge and Harry Williams in Stalybridge in 1912, "It's a Long Way to Tipperary," became a marching anthem on the battlefields of Europe. See http://www.stalybridge.org.uk/history.htm (accessed Oct. 25, 2008).

[10] "He would be eleven years old. Child labor laws were still in the future." G. Homer Durham, in MS 7644, footnote 2, 2. Studies show that "The share of children in the cotton mill workforce actually fell sharply in the half century before

to work for Robt Brigley & Co (until they broke up which was the latter end of the same year) on account of them giving me 2 shillings per week more.[11]

[In Dec. 1843] Jonathan Mills came for me to go and work for him again and he said he would give me 1 shilling more per week if my father would let me go again. So my father consented for me to go and I went to the saw when I cut my thumb & first and second fingers very bad indeed so that I had to play me 1 month through it.[12]  Got to my work again but did not saw any more but started to work on a lathe to learn the trade. Did so till April 1844 when he wanted my father to let me be bound-Prentice with him. In May my father gave consent. I should have been bound on the 2nd (it being my birthday) but the indentures were not quite ready so it was put off until the 9th of May 1844 when I was bound Prentice to Jonathan Mills for the term of 5 years to learn the bobbin and skewer turning trade (by George Taylor,

---

significant legislative restrictions on child labor. In a survey in 1788, 'children' made up two-thirds of the workforce on powered equipment in 143 water mills in England and Scotland. A survey of 982 mills in England and Scotland in 1835, before the Factory Act of 1833 had fully taken effect, indicated that 43% of the workforce was under eighteen . . . . The share of cotton mill workers under eighteen in surveys in Manchester, Stockport, and Preston in 1816-9 were 47%, 58%, and 65% respectively, while by 1835 the corresponding figures had fallen to 39%, 36%, and 47% . . . . The image of dark satanic mills consuming children is a central image of the Industrial Revolution. Life for a child laborer in the early English factories was brutal. Nonetheless, some children not only endured but went on to become adult factory workers." Douglas A. Galbi, "Child Labor and the Division of Labor in the Early English Cotton Mills," Journal of Population Economics, Vol 10, No. 4, 1997, 1,3. Available at SSRN: http://ssrn.com/abstract=42388 (accessed March 24, 2009).

[11] "His wage from Jonathan Mills is not disclosed, possibly ten shillings?" G. Homer Durham, in MS 7644, footnote 3, 2.

[12] "Despite the loss of these fingers he learned to play the reed organ." G. Homer Durham, in MS 7644, footnote 4, 2.

solicitor of Staylybridge): to have 8 shillings per week the first and second years, 10s the third, 11s the fourth and 13s the 5th and last year. We agreed very well the first, second, and third years. But the fourth and fifth years (were) not so comfortable because he wanted to bate me for all my lost time but my father would not allow it. Therefore we had a deal of uneasiness. We had threatened law once or twice before he would pay me my wages according to his own agreement but afterwards was very comfortable. On the 9th of May 1849 I was loose,[13] my time being up and served. I told him so. He told me to go on with my work as usual so I did as he told me and the week following I began on Journeyman's which was 22s a week. At that time trade not being so good at that time, stayed with him until November in the same year when I left him to go and work for Richard Jackson as he had got some very large orders in. So I stayed with him until those were finished.

On the first of May 1849 I was baptized by Elder William Thorley of Dukinfield[14] and on Sunday the 6th of May Elder Thorley confirmed

---

[13] "Free of his apprenticeship." G. Homer Durham, in MS 7644, footnote 5, p. 3.

[14] Dukinfield is a small town within Tameside, in Greater Manchester, England. "It lies approximately seven miles (11 km) to the east of the City of Manchester. Historically a part of Cheshire, the town is a product of the Industrial Revolution when its development was accelerated by the growth of coal mining and the cotton industry. "The name of this municipal borough probably means 'ducks' open-land', although it is traditionally taken to commemorate a victory of Saxons over Danish invaders. [The] enormous growth of industry, especially the cotton trade, had the most profound effect on the people of Dukinfield. A contemporary observer said of the cotton trade in 1794 that 'while it affords employment to all ages, it has debilitated the constitutions and retarded the growth of many, and made an alarming increase in the mortality.' The rural aspect of Dukinfield was quickly marred and finally destroyed. After an absence of nearly 60 years the missionary Robert Moffat returned to Dukinfield in 1875 and wept at the sight. 'What a difference. What a change! My heart almost broke when I thought of the past and compared it with the present.' Poorly managed industrial change led to social disturbances, including the widespread industrial riots of 1812 (the Luddite Riots) and 1842 (the Plug Riots).

me a member of the Church of Jesus Christ of Latter day Saints.[15] I was then keeping company with a female of the name of Mary Morton and had been for some time previous to this. I was also conducting the singing at the time in the Dukinfield Branch and had been for about 2 years previous to being baptized.

On the 22nd of October 1849 I was married to Mary Morton at Hollinwood[16] near Oldham, Lancashire in the presence of my sister Sarah and her husband & others. Mary Morton my wife was born at Stalybridge, Lancashire on the 30th of January 1829. She is the daughter of Joshua and Harriet Morton. Joshua was born at _____, in _____ on ____ the ___ of 1803. Harriet was born at _____ in _____ on the _____ of _____. They were married at Manchester[17] on the

There were also riots in 1858, 1863 and 1868." See http://www.tameside.gov .uk/dukinfield/history (accessed Oct. 25, 2008).

[15] "At 21 years of age." G. Homer Durham, in MS 7644, footnote 6, 3.

[16] Hollinwood is in an area of southwest Oldham, in Greater Manchester, England. Historically a part of Lancashire, Hollinwood was formerly a village within the township of Chadderton.

[17] Historically, most of the city, Manchester, was a part of Lancashire, with areas south of the River Mersey being in Cheshire. It is said that Manchester was the world's first industrialized city and it played a dominant role during the Industrial Revolution. It was the international center of textile manufacture and cotton spinning and received the nickname Cottonopolis. "The transformation from a market town to a major city began in 1761 when the . . . canal began to bring cheap coal to Manchester. By the end of the 18th century Manchester had established itself as the centre of the cotton industry in Lancashire. The merchants brought the raw cotton from Liverpool, sold it to small-time masters in Manchester who then passed it to the spinners working in the cottages. In the 1770s the invention of machines such as the Spinning Jenny and the Water Frame completely changed the way that cotton goods were produced. The machines in the first textile factories were driven by water-power and were therefore built in villages besides fast-flowing streams. By 1790 there were about a hundred and fifty water-powered cotton spinning factories in Britain. Richard Arkwright was quick to see the significance of the Rotary Steam-Engine invented by James Watt and in 1783 he began using the machine in his Cromford factory. Others followed his lead and by 1800 there were over 500 of

____ of ____ and resided at Stalybridge when they had a daughter (which they named Mary) on the 30th of January 1829. And on the 17th of June 1831 they had another daughter, named Sarah and on the

---

Watt's machines in Britain's mines and factories. With the invention of Watt's steam-engine, factories no longer had to be built close to fast-flowing rivers and streams. Entrepreneurs now tended to build factories where there was a good supply of labour and coal. Manchester became the obvious place to build textile factories. Large warehouses were also built to store and display the spun yarn and finished cloth. The town's population grew rapidly. With neighbouring Salford, Manchester had about 25,000 inhabitants in 1772. By 1800 the population had grown to 95,000. The rich manufacturers built large houses around the Mosley Street area. At first the cheap housing for the factory workers were confined to New Cross and Newtown. However, as the population grew, close-packed houses were built next to factories all over Manchester." See Medieval British Towns, "Manchester," http://www.spartacus.schoolnet.co.uk/ITmanchester.htm (accessed March 26, 2009). "Despite the growing wealth due to trade and commerce, prosperity lay in the hands of very few of Manchester's residents. The working people, who actually produced the wealth, lived, worked and died in conditions of the most desperate poverty and degradation. Innumerable reports and surveys were carried out during the 19th century, and they all told much the same story: poor wages, impossibly long working hours, dangerous and unsanitary working conditions, even more unsanitary dwellings, little or no health provisions, high infant mortality and a short life expectancy. A map of Manchester showing age of death figures in the mid-nineteenth century revealed that life expectancy was directly related to wealth. Put simply, the poor died younger and the rich lived longer. At that time, Ancoats was the black death spot of Manchester. Records show that by 1830 there were over 560 cotton mills in Lancashire, employing more than 110,000 workers, of which 35,000 were children - some as young as six years of age. Wages for children were about 2s.3d. (two shillings and three pence) per week (about 11½ new pence), but adults were paid about 10 times more. Hence, it made economic sense to employ as many children and as few adults as possible, and this is exactly what happened. Youngest children were employed to crawl beneath machinery (while still in operation) to gather up loose cotton—they were known as 'scavengers' and many died by getting caught up in machinery. Those that survived to adulthood had permanent stoops or were crippled from the prolonged crouching that the job entailed. The typical working day was 14 hours long, but many were much longer, as, without regulation, unscrupulous mill owners could demand any terms they liked." See Manchester UK, "History and Heritage," http://www.manchester2002-uk.com/history.html (accessed March 26, 2009).

___ of ____ they had a son which they named Joseph; and on the ___ of ____ they had another son which they called William; and on the 23rd of Nov 1835 they had a daughter which they called Eliza.

On the 10 of June 1835 Joshua their father died, aged 32 and was interred at Stalybridge. All their children were born at Stalybridge. Sarah their daughter died on the ___ of ____. Joseph their son died on the ___ of ____. William their son died on the ___ of ____. All were interred at Stalybridge.[18]

Mary and Eliza, after the death of their father, lived with Joseph and Mary Schofield who were Harriet's father and mother. But after we were married we went to live with my sister Sarah in Dukinfield where we stayed till January 1850. We then removed to Stalybridge on account of it being nearer our work -&c-.

Mary my wife was baptized on the 10th of Aug. 1845 by David Swift and was confirmed a member of the Church of Jesus Christ of Latter day Saints in Dukinfield by Elder Joseph Slinger on the 11th of Aug. 1845.

Eliza my wife's youngest sister was baptized on the ___ of ____ by Elder Wm. Thorley and was confirmed a member of the Church of Jesus Christ of Latter day Saints by Elder Wm. Thorley on the___ of ____ at Stalybridge.

About March 1851 I began to teach a singing class at Bro. Shipley's in Newton according to the request of some of the brethren and sisters of the Hyde Branch.[19] We met on a Sunday morning for

---

[18] "They evidently died at early ages and Thomas did not know the dates." G. Homer Durham, in MS 7644, footnote 7, 4.

[19] Hyde, Cheshire County. The Metropolitan Borough of Tameside is a metropolitan borough (county) of Greater Manchester in North West England. It is named after the River Tame which flows through the borough and consists of the nine towns of Ashton, Audenshaw, Denton, Droylsden, Dukinfield, Hyde, Longdendale, Mossley and Stalybridge. Its western border is approximately four miles east of Manchester city center. It borders Derbyshire to the east, the Metropolitan Borough of Oldham to

that purpose at 8 o clock, but still continued to conduct the singing at Stalybridge.

On Sun. the 7th of Sep. 1851, Elder John Albiston called and ordained me to the office of a Priest in the Stalybridge Branch.[20] And about October in the same year I began to teach a singing class at Mottram[21] in Bro. Whiting's house on Sunday forenoons after I had been to Newton.[22] I preached several times in the Foresters Hall,[23] Stalybridge, up to the 2 of May 1852 when I was appointed to go with Elder Bradley from Hyde and Brother Done of the Ashton Branch to preach in the open air at Glossop[24] for 1 month which we did. But it

---

the north, the Metropolitan Borough of Stockport to the south, and the City of Manchester to the west. "The town owes its importance to the cotton manufacture, and possesses weaving factories, spinning-mills, print works, iron-foundries, and machine-works." See *The Encyclopedia Britannica*, 9th ed., (Philadelphia: J.M. Stoddart, 1884) s.v. "Hyde," 442.

[20] "At age 23, four months, and five days." G. Homer Durham, in MS 7644, footnote 8, 5.

[21] Located southeast of Stalybridge.

[22] "Newton is located near the intersection of an old road between Haydock and Lowton, and a Roman road from Warrington to Wigan, and probably got its name during Saxon times when it emerged, simply as a 'new town.' However, excavations at Castle Hill in Newton have revealed ancient British artifacts dating back to 55 BC and suggest that it was constructed by the Celts as a burial mound." See Manchester UK, "The County of Lancashire," http://www.manchester2002-uk.com/lancashire-towns-4.html (accessed March 22, 2009).

[23] The principal public buildings in Stalybridge were the town hall (1831), the Foresters' Hall (1836), the district infirmary, the mechanics' institute (1861), the people's institute (1864), the market-hall (1866, and the Oddfellows' hall (1878). *The Encyclopedia Britannica*, 9th ed., (Philadelphia: J.M. Stoddart, 1884) s.v. "Stalybridge," 446.

[24] Glossop, Derbyshire was a bustling mill town and because of an abundant water supply "in the late 18th and early 19th centuries no less than 46 mills were built in this period." See "Peak District Information," http://www.cressbrook.co.uk/towns/glossop.php (accessed Mar. 22, 2009).

was a hard task to me, it being the first time that ever I stood up in the open air to speak. We met with opposition, the first Sunday we went, from a primitive Methodist preacher in Edward Street. He called us for murderers and thieves and everything that was bad. We met with opposition every Sunday. During that month I was also appointed clerk for the council of the outdoor missions and was appointed to Glossop again for the month of June, along with Bro. S. Austin and Bro. Done, where we went and met with opposition every time we went, and every time we preached, especially in Edward Street where Mr. Robert Lowe and Jonathan Billclif opposed us strenuously every time we went. Elder Wm. Thorley was with us once or twice there and met with a warm reception as they termed it. We had very good and attentive congregations every time we preached in Glossop.

July 11th, which was the council at Mottram for the outdoor missions, but Bro. Schofield the prest of the Stalybridge Branch desired me to stay at the Branch Council of Stalybridge which I did. Financial business was settled then. Pres. Schofield said that there (was) wanted a man appointed to lay hands on for the recovery of the sick, one that they could rely on for that purpose. President Schofield moved that Elder James Lord be released from the Prest'cy of the No. 1 District of the Stalybridge Branch and that he be the individual for the saints to look to when they are sick, both for the No. 1 and No. 2 Districts of this branch. Pres. Schofield then said that there (was) wanted a man appointed to preside over the No. 1 District in Bro. Lord's stead. He then moved, which was secd by Elder J.W. Payson, that I took the charge of the No. 1 District which then numbered about 36 saints which I felt to be a heavy load upon my shoulders, with but being young in the Priesthood. I was appointed at the Mottram council to go to Glossop[25] for another month with the same brethren which I

---

[25] Located southeast of Mottram in Derbyshire County.

did but we still continued to meet with a good deal of opposition. I used to leave my home about 8 o'clock in the morning and get back about 9 or 10 o'clock at night and some times later than that. Several times we have begun to preach in Edward Street about 5 o'clock and have been there while 9 o'clock and in the rain all the time, once or twice, and then had to walk home which is about 8 miles. But the Lord was always with us to bless us in time of need. We used to go up into a small wood to eat our dinners where we knelt down to ask the blessing of our Heavenly Father upon us through the day.

The District meetings were then held at our house on Wednesday evenings over which I had to preside. I was also on the tract committee which met every other Tuesday night which I attended, regularly. The Branch councils were held every other Sat. night which I also attended.

Saturday night, August 5th, went to the monthly council at Mottram. The meeting was opened as usual with prayer. When I was called upon to represent the Glossop mission, as our Prest S. Austen had not been with us once this month, the Prest moved that I went to Charlsworth,[26] Fattinghay,[27] &c for one month in company with Bro. S. Connell and James Quayle. On Sunday the 15th, we went through New York where I preached a little and bore my testimony. Afterwards Elder Thorley spoke as he had come with us this day to

---

[26] "Charlesworth is a pretty village nestling on the side of the Pennines, 12 miles north of Buxton and south of Mottram. It lies on the borders of three Shires, Lancashire, Yorkshire and Cheshire but is part of Derbyshire. The cotton mills established in the 19th century have long since ceased to operate but the village has two rows of small cottages where the occupants used to weave cotton, many of the cottages possessing third storey rooms where this cottage industry took place. The weavers would have gone down Long Lane over the packhorse Best Hill Bridge to Manchester for their supplies." See http://www.derbyshireuk.net/charlesworth.html (accessed Oct. 25, 2008).

[27] No information on Fattinghay.

meet a gentleman at Fattinghay who had opposed the brethren before, and told them he would be there again. As today we began to preach at Fattinghay, about 5 o'clock (opposite Bro. Houndfarels door) he came and began to oppose Bro. Thorley. So we stayed till dark, then came away and left them as we had a long way to walk home. Got home about 10 o'clock.

On Thursday night, 26th, I went with Brothers Thorley and Whittaker to Tintwistle[28] to hear the Rev. Mr. Chalmers deliver a lecture against Mormonism. After he had done, Bro. Thorley rose up to make a reply to some things that he had stated (about 30 or 40 present).

On Sunday the 29th I went to the Ashton[29] District conference. Was there all day. Sister Durham, my wife, was with me. September was not any meeting for the outdoor missions, so we all continued as we were without any alternative.

Sunday 5th, went to Fattinghay &c as usual with the brethren. I preached at Fattinghay.

On Friday night Sep 10th I baptized Jessed Goodfellow at Stalybridge.

On Sunday the 12th I went with the brethren to Fattinghay &c. Sister Durham, Sister Connell and Sister Howarth were with us. After dinner we went up on the couns. Rocks Derbyshire.[30] It being very

---

[28] Tintwistle is a village in the county of Derbyshire, England. The village is just north of Glossop at the lower end of the Longdendale valley. It lies within the historic county boundaries of Cheshire.

[29] Ashton Hayes is a village and civil parish in the Chester District of Cheshire, England. It is located about 8 miles east of Chester. The nearest villages are Mouldsworth to the north east and Kelsall to the south east. The main village in the parish was formerly known as Ashton.

[30] This could refer to the Black Rocks area, a small outcrop of natural grit stone, located between Cromford and Wirksworth, situated in the Derbyshire Peak District. The area has been a well-known rock climbing venue since the 1890s.

windy we did not stay long.  Got back about 5 o'clock and had a church meeting in Bro. Handfords house, it being too cold to preach out of doors.

On Sunday the 19th I was released from the outdoor mission so that I could attend to the singing and look after the saints that I then presided over. It was Prest Schofield's desire, not mine, so on this day I was at the room at Stalybridge.[31]

On Sunday Sep 26th the room at Stalybridge was closed.  So me and Sister Durham went to Sheffield[32] to see Bro. and Sister Albiston according to their request (Brother Albiston was then presiding over the Sheffield conference).  We got there about ½ past 10 o'clock. Sister Albiston was at the station waiting for the train coming in.  It was conference day so we went to the room all day, had dinner and tea[33] at Bro. Albistons, slept there at night.

On Monday the 27th we went with a party of the Sheffield saints to Wharncliff rocks.[34]  We had a Brass Band with us but had not much

---

[31] "The meeting places of the Saints were generally called 'the room' or 'rooms,' and for many years, into the 20th century, were rented facilities. G. Homer Durham, in MS 7644, footnote 9, 8.

[32] "This travel would be by the early railroad systems of Britain." G. Homer Durham, in MS 7644 footnote 10, 8. Sheffield is a city in Yorkshire, 39 miles south of Leeds. It was named after the River Sheaf that runs through the city. "Sheffield was . . . the chief seat of the cutlery trade in England. The prosperity of Sheffield is chiefly dependent on the manufacture of steel . . . . The smelting of iron . . . is supposed to date back as far as the Norman Conquest. The town had become famed for its cutlery by the 14th century, as is shown by allusions in Chaucer [in *The Canterbury Tales*]." *The Encyclopedia Britannica*, 9th ed., (Philadelphia: J.M. Stoddart, 1884) s.v. "Sheffield," 882-884. Innovations in crucible and stainless steel fueled an astounding increase in the population during the Industrial Revolution. Mary, Queen of Scots, was held prisoner at Sheffield Castle from 1570 to 1584.

[33] "The English snack, usually about 4 or 5 p.m." G. Homer Durham, in MS 7644, footnote 11, 8.

[34] Wharncliffe Crags is a gritstone escarpment or edge situated approximately six miles northwest of the city of Sheffield. Quern stones have been quarried from this

pleasure because it rained and blew all day so that we had to be under shelter. We got back to Sheffield about 8 o'clock, slept at Bro. Albiston's again.

On Tuesday the 28th, Brother Albiston took us through Sheffield and to Brother Whitbys where we stayed to dinner, he having a pianoforte I enjoyed myself first rate.[35] After dinner Sister Albiston came. We stayed there till 4 o'clock then went to Bro. Abel's to tea according to promise. There we enjoyed ourselves very well in singing the songs of Zion, after which we went to Bro. Albiston's and stayed the night. It was very stormy and wet all day.

On Wednesday morning the 29th we left Sheffield on the 8 o'clock train for Mottram station. Bro. Albiston came with us. We walked from Mottram to Stalybridge. We called at Bro. Thos. Haworths and had dinner with them, then came forward to Stalybridge.

On the 14th of April 1852 my sister Mary Ann died of a fever and was interred on the 17th at the Wesleyan Chapel, Stalybridge.[36] She was in her 16th year.[37]

---

area as far back as the Iron Age and into the Roman occupation of Great Britain. The name Wharn is a derivation of "quern."

[35] "By this time he was 24 years of age." G. Homer Durham, in MS 7644, footnote 12, 9.

[36] Stalybridge, Methodist Chapel (Wesleyan), Caroline Street. Founded 1762, built 1815, rebuilt 1872. Registers 1812-1837 are at Lancashire Record Office. See http://www.ukbmd.org.uk/ genuki/chs/stalybridge.html (accessed March 22, 2009).

[37] "Thomas Durham, now nearing his 24th birthday, framed this entry in a rectangular 'box' drawn in his journal." G. Homer Durham, in MS 7644, footnote 13, 9.

On Sunday the 3rd of Oct was at the room all day and at night I preached.

On Wed the 6<sup>th</sup> I went with Brother Wm.Thorley and James Lord to a[n] open council meeting at Hyde when charges were said against Wm Potts the Pres't of the Branch for lieing and keeping company with young women but nothing was proved against him clearly. Elder James Whitworth presided.

On Wednesday night the 13<sup>th</sup> I went to Hyde again to hear the same case tried with Elder Jonathan Midgley the Pres't of the Manchester conference. Nothing proved against him but Elder Midgley removed him from the Presidency of the Branch and put Elder Charles Kemp in his stead. This was done for the well being of the Branch generally.

Sunday the 17<sup>th</sup> at the room all day.

Sunday the 24<sup>th</sup> at the room all day. Preached in the evening.

Sunday the 31st at the room all the day.

Sunday the 7<sup>th</sup> Nov. at the room

On Thursday night the 11<sup>th</sup> went with Bros. S. Whittaker to a[n] open council in the room opposite the Carpenters Hall,[38] Manchester to hear the case of Sam'l Hawthornwaite reheard (he having been cut off by the Manchester Branch for spreading evil, so he applied to the Presidency at Liverpool to have his case reheard and it was granted). Pres't S.W. Richards presided. The case was tried and then Pres't Richards said that the Manchester council had acted right in cutting him off and told them to let him remain out of the Church until he repented.

On Sunday night the 14<sup>th</sup> I preached at Stalybridge.

---

[38] Carpenters' Hall was built when carpenters contributed union funds and this building was used for various functions and gatherings, including meetings held by members of The Church of Jesus Christ of Latter-day Saints. See http://www.chartists.net/Manchester-Chartists.htm (accessed March 22, 2009).

Sunday the 21$^{st}$ went to the District conference held in the Foresters Hall, Stalybridge. Elder Whitworth presided, Elders Wheelock and Midgley were present and addressed the meeting.

In the afternoon Elder Wheelock called me to the office of an elder, and on Tuesday, the 23$^{rd}$, went to the Ashton room when Elder Wheelock ordained me to that office.

On Sunday the 28$^{th}$ at the room.

On Sunday the 5 of Dec., the Stalybridge Branch held a fast day until 6 o'clock at night. Forenoon had a prayer meeting, afternoon had a testimony meeting. The Spirit of the Lord was with us all day and we felt to rejoice under its influence. I bore my testimony to the work of God. After I sat down Sist(er) Mary Wood rose upon her feet and spoke a prophecy upon me and told me many things which have literally come to pass.

Sunday Dec. 12$^{th}$ at the room all day and in the evening I preached a short time on the subject of immediate revelation from God.

Wednesday 15$^{th}$ night at the meeting as usual.

Saturday night the 18$^{th}$ I baptized 3 girls, viz. Sarah Whittaker, Hannah Walker and Ann Schofield at Stalybridge. The weather was very severe and cold.

Sunday, 19$^{th}$ at the room. In the afternoon Pres't Schofield desired me to confirm Sister Sarah Slinger, senior, and Ann Schofield which I attended unto.

On Sunday the 16$^{th}$ of January 1853 I attended a conference of the Ashton District which was held in Foresters Hall, Stalybridge, when Elders Wheelock and Midgley were present and the following elders from the valley,[39] namely H. Cook, O.M. Duel, P.G. Sessions, and W.

---

[39] "Possibly he meant the Salt Lake Valley." G. Homer Durham, in MS 7644, footnote 14, 11.

Treat.   They all spoke some little concerning their mission to this land[40] which was very pleasing and interesting.

On Wednesday night the 19th I went with Bro. Joseph Paramore to Pres't J. Schofields at Droylsden[41] to have a blessing from Elder [Cyrus] Wheelock.[42] My blessing was as follows:

"Dear Brother Thos.   I tell thee in the name of the Lord Jesus Christ that thou shall begin from this time to have more power to do good and thy labours shall be blessed of thy father in heaven more than heretofore they have been, and thy brethren and sisters will cling round thee in the hour of affliction and sorrow and in a few years from this time thou shall be in the land of Zion with thy wife.  Thou shall be called to a quorum of seventies and thou shall be blessed greatly of the Lord thy God because of thy purity and faithfulness, and thy sons shall fight the battles of the Lord when God and Magog shall rise up against the Lord of hosts.  And if thou art faithful not a stain shall come upon thee nor thy seed throughout all eternity.

---

[40] "England."  G. Homer Durham, in MS 7644, footnote 15, 11.

[41] Another town in Tameside, in the historic county of Lancashire. "The origins of the township are obscure. Some believe that it existed in the 7th century AD, but it was probably first mentioned by name in 1250. There are various interpretations of the meaning of the name. It could mean Drygel's valley—'Drygel' being a companion of war—or dry valley or dry spring—'dryge' being Old English for dry. The population in 1831 was 3,000, by 1861 it had risen to 8,000 and in 1900 it was 11,000. The first terry towel—the first machine woven towel in the world was produced in Droylsden in a specially adapted loom." See Tameside.gov.uk/ "Township Information – Droylsden," http://www.tameside.gov.uk/droylsden /history (accessed March 22, 2009).

[42] "Patriarch."  G. Homer Durham, in MS 7644, footnote 16, 11.  Cyrus Wheelock was second counselor to Franklin D. Richards (President of the European Mission and member of the Quorum of the Twelve Apostles), and composer of the words to the hymn, "Ye Elders of Israel," *Hymns* (Salt Lake City: The Church of Jesus Christ of Latter-day Saints, 1985) no. 319.

"And when thou shall rise up to speak to the people thy ideas shall be clear and thou shall have language to clothe them with and thou shall be an instrument in the hand of the Lord thy God of bringing many souls to a knowledge of the truth and many shall call thee blessed because of thy purity and thy name shall be revered through all the earth.

"Thy attainments in music shall be great and thou will be loved in Zion and in her stakes because of the heavenly strains that thou will bring forth, and angels shall reveal and sing unto thee, while laid upon thy pillow, the songs that are sung in the heavens above. Thou shalt also sing and rejoice in the temple of the most high God and attend unto the ordinances for the living and the dead.

"Be faithful Dear Brother and these blessings are thine with all that are laid up for the faithful in the name of the Lord Jesus Christ. Amen."

Sunday the 23$^{rd}$ at the room all day.

On Sunday the 6$^{th}$ of February was at the room and preached in the evening.

Sat'y night the 12$^{th}$ went to Mottram to the monthly council of the Stalybridge District. Brother Schofield, president, opened the meeting with prayer after which I was appointed president of the Mottram Branch on account of Elder Haworth emigrating and Elder John Cowdell was appointed my councilor and to act as pres't of the Branch until such times as Pres. Schofield could spare me from the Stalybridge Branch.

Sunday the 13$^{th}$ at the room all day.

Sunday the 27$^{th}$ preached in the Foresters Hall in the evening.

On the 20$^{th}$ I went with Bro. Schofield to the room at Tintwistle and we had a very good meeting. Got home about 8 o'clock. It was very fine all day.

On the 6$^{th}$, 13$^{th}$ and 20 of March at the room.

On Sunday the 27th went to the Manchester conference. Stayed all day, Sister Durham was with me and Eliza Morton her sister.

Sunday, April 3rd at the room and ordained Bro. Wm. Morris[43] to the office of a teacher.

Sun. the 10th at the room all day.

On Sunday the 17th at the room and preached at night.

Sun'y the 24th at the room.

On Saturday night the 30th a tea party was held in the Foresters Hall for the benefit of the Sunday School. Elder Sessions was with us. After tea recitations were given and the choir sang some favorite glees and a selection from *Uncle Tom's Cabin*.[44] Elder Sessions stayed at our house.

On Sunday the 1st of May the Stalybridge District Conference was held in the Foresters Hall, Stalybridge, Elder Schofield presiding. In the evening Elder Sessions preached to a large congregation. He stayed all night at our house and Elder Schofield also.

Wednesday night the 4th went to the meeting, spoke a short time to the saints.

---

[43] This would be William Morris, Thomas' brother-in-law (married to Sarah Durham.) "William Morris was born 6 Nov 1820 to Joseph Morris and Elizabeth Vernon at Burswardsley, Cheshire, England. He had a small shop in England but when he came to Parowan he did any kind of work he could find to make a living . . . . [He] was a very kind, honest man, possessed a cheerful disposition . . . [and] was loved and respected by all, his neighbors and especially his family." See Cora M. Rowley, "Life Story of William Morris as remembered and sought out by his grandaughter [sic] Cora M. Rowley" (Cedar City, UT, n.p., n.d., photocopy of typescript), 85-86.

[44] The internationally known American novel, written by Harriet Beecher Stowe, which used the real life contributions of Rev. Josiah Henson in the Underground Railroad as the basis of her creation of the character Uncle Tom in the 1852 protest against slavery.

On Saturday night the 7th went to the monthly council at Mottram when brethren were appointed to go into the open air to preach the gospel. Elder William Thorley to preside over them.

On Sunday the 8th I was at the room.

Wednesday night the 11th went to the meeting.

Sunday the 15th went to Tintwistle in company with Sister Durham and Eliza, her sister, to Brother Wm. Whitings. Took dinner with them, went to meeting in the afternoon, took tea with them then came to Mottram room at night when Elder Cowdell asked me to preach which I did for a short time on the necessity of divine revelation in our day.

Wednesday 18th started from Stalybridge to go to Bangor on a pleasure trip. Took lodgings in High Street – Bangor. [45]

Thursday 19th crossed the ferry to Beawmauris castle built in 1200, destroyed by Oliver Cromwell. [46]

---

[45] Bangor, a town, in Gwynedd, NW Wales, at the northern end of Menai Strait. "Bangor has a proud history which can be traced back to 525 AD when Deiniol, a Celtic missionary, established a monastic community on the site of the present cathedral. For centuries it remained a small town of two streets, with the cathedral as its focal point, and few positive signs of expansion. The second half of the nineteenth century saw Bangor firmly established as the most important town in north Wales. New shops and three banks were opened in the High Street . . . ." See BBC Home, Wales North West "Bangor," http://www.bbc.co.uk/wales/northwest/ sites/history/pages/ growthofbangor.shtml (accessed March 22, 2009). "High Street" was the expression for the main retail or business center or of the city. The claim was made that Bangor allegedly had the longest High Street in Wales.

[46] "Beaumaris, begun in 1295, was the last and largest of the castles to be built by King Edward I in Wales. Raised on an entirely new site, without earlier buildings to fetter its designer's creative genius, it is possibly the most sophisticated example of medieval military architecture in Britain. This is undoubtedly the ultimate 'concentric castle, built with an almost geometric symmetry. Conceived as an integral whole, a high inner ring of defenses is surrounded by a lower outer circuit of walls, combining an almost unprecedented level of strength and firepower. Before the age of cannon, the attacker would surely have been faced with an impregnable fortress. Yet, ironically, the work of construction was never fully completed, and the castle saw little action apart from the Civil War in the 17th century. A castle was

Friday 20th went to see the Menai Bridge which is suspended with chains across Menai Straits[47] and also saw the Britannia tubular Bridge 600 yards through,[48] and other things very curious.

---

almost certainly planned when King Edward visited Anglesey in 1283 and designated the Welsh town of Llanfaes to be its seat of government. At the time, resources were already stretched and any such scheme was postponed. Then, in 1294-95, the Welsh rose in revolt under Madog ap Llywelyn. The rebels were crushed after an arduous winter campaign, and the decision was taken to proceed with a new castle in April 1295. The extent of English power is demonstrated by the fact that the entire native population of Llanfaes was forced to move to a newly established settlement, named Newborough. The castle itself was begun on the 'fair marsh,' and was given the Norman-French name Beau Mareys. Building progressed at an astonishing speed, with some 2,600 men engaged in the work during the first year." See http://www.castlewales.com/beaumar.html (accessed March 24, 2009).

[47] "White Knight says to Alice, 'I heard him then, for I had just completed my design. / To keep the Menai Bridge from rust. / By boiling it in wine.'" (Lewis Carroll, *Through the Looking Glass*, Chapter VIII) "Traffic across the strait and Anglesey increased in the early 19th century after the Act of Union of 1800, when Ireland joined the United Kingdom. Travelers to the ferry port of Holyhead, where ships left for Ireland, had to make the dangerous crossing after a long and arduous journey from London. Soon plans were drawn up by Thomas Telford for ambitious improvements to the route from London to Holyhead, including a bridge over the Menai. One of the design requirements for the bridge was that it needed to have 100 feet of clear space under the main span, to allow for the passage of the tall sailing ships that plied the strait. This was done by designing a suspension bridge, with sixteen massive chains holding up a 579 foot length of road surface between the two towers. Although small suspension bridges had been built before, none approached the scale that Telford proposed for this one. Despite much opposition from the ferry owners and tradesmen in the ports, construction of the bridge started in 1819. The stone used for the arches and piers was limestone quarried from Penmon Quarries at the north end of the strait, then carried down by boat. The ironwork came from Hazeldean's foundry near Shrewsbury. To prevent the iron from rusting between production and use on the bridge, the iron was immersed, not in boiling wine as the White Knight suggested above, but in warm linseed oil. The stonework was finished in 1824; then began the monumental task of raising the chains that would hold up the central span. Tunnels were driven into solid rock on either shore to anchor the chains. Then the first section of the chain was secured on the Caernarfonshire side, drawn up to the top of the eastern tower and left to hang down to the water level. Another chain was drawn up to the top of the tower on the Anglesey side. The

central section of chain, weighing 23.5 tons, was then loaded onto a raft, carefully maneuvered into position between the towers and connected to the dangling chain. While a fife and drum band played to encourage the workers, 150 men used block and tackle to draw the chain up to the top of the Anglesey tower to complete the span. The large crowd that had gathered to watch cheered wildly as the connection was made. The remaining fifteen chains were raised in a similar manner over the next ten weeks. Rods were then hung from the chains and bolted to iron bars that were used as the base for the wooden road surface. The bridge was opened on 30 January 1826 to great fanfare. Its completion, along with other improvements to the road by Telford, reduced travel time from London to Holyhead from 36 hours to 27 (today it takes 5.5 hours)." See http://www.anglesey-history.co.uk/places/bridges/ (accessed Nov. 22, 2008).

[48] "The completion of the Menai Bridge was a boon in easing the journey to the island, particularly for travel to Ireland. However, the rapid rise of rail travel later in the 19th century meant that there was soon a need for trains to cross the Strait. When plans were first being made to build a railway to Holyhead it was proposed that the carriages be taken over the Menai Bridge; the carriages would be uncoupled from the locomotive at one end, then drawn across one by one, using horses, to a waiting locomotive at the other end. This idea was abandoned and plans were drawn up for a new bridge, the Britannia, by Robert Stephenson, son of the locomotive pioneer George Stephenson. He faced the challenge of building a bridge rigid and strong enough to carry a heavy train of many carriages. This was done by making the bridge out of two long iron tubes, rectangular in shape, through which the trains would travel. When first conceived, the tubular bridge was to have been suspended from cables strung through the openings at the tops of the towers. However, after engineering calculations and tests of the finished tubes it was decided that they were strong enough by themselves to carry the trains. Stephenson faced a much greater challenge in raising the 1,500 ton finished tubes than had Telford with his much lighter chains. He too would float the tube into position. However, the process didn't go as smoothly with the first tube as with the Menai Bridge chains and the giant tube came close to being swept out to sea. Fortune prevailed and it did finally end up in place. Then, very slowly, using hydraulic pumps, the tube was raised into position. Stonework was built up under the ends of the tube as it was lifted; this was to support it if the lifting equipment failed. This was fortunate because one pump did indeed fail, but the tube only fell nine inches. With the tubes in place the final touches were added. These are the four magnificent limestone lions that guard the entrances to the bridge. They were carved by John Thomas, who had also done stone carving for the Houses of Parliament and Buckingham Palace in London. The lions are almost 4 meters high and sit on plinths of equal height. The bridge was opened on 5 March

Saturday 21st stayed at Chester[49] all night.

Sunday 22nd got home about 12 o'clock, preached at the Foresters Hall at night. In the afternoon bore my testimony.

Sunday June 5th ½ past 12 o'clock, went to the meeting and bore my testimony, after which Sister Mary Wood spoke the following prophecy which was interpreted by Bro. Thos. Lord as follows:

"Dear Brother Thomas: I tell thee by that Spirit which has long cemented us together and caused us to love one another in the name of Jesus Christ. I say unto thee, fret not thyself but be cheerful before the Lord they God, for he shall bless thee. And thou shall see those prophecies immediately fulfilled which have been spoken concerning thee. Thou will have to do a great work for the Lord in these lands for many shall believe thy words and obey the gospel and go to Zion with thee and then thou shalt attain higher in the Priesthood through which thou shalt work signs and wonders and miracles in the midst of the earth.[50]

"Thou will have to go to nations unknown to the inhabitants around thee and thou will be brought before rulers and kings of the earth and will be bound hand and foot (like the Apostle Paul), and cast into prison for the gospel's sake.

---

1850." See http://www.anglesey-history.co.uk/ places/bridges/ (accessed Nov. 22, 2008).

[49] Chester is located in the county of Cheshire, England, lying on the River Dee, close to the border with Wales. "Founded by the Romans over 2000 years ago, much of the Roman influence remains and Chester's city walls are the most complete in Britain. In every corner of the city you are confronted with history, from the Roman amphitheatre, which is currently under excavation [2009], to the medieval half-timbered buildings. Chester Cathedral was founded as a Benedictine monastery over 900 years ago and attracts hundreds of thousand visitors per year." See "Chester" http://www.chester.com/visitchester/aboutchester/ (accessed March 22, 2009).

[50] "He became Patriarch of the Parowan Stake in his later years." G. Homer Durham, in MS 7644, footnote 17, 14.

"And thou shalt be blessed with the seed that has been promised thee, yea, with a great and mighty seed and shall go to tribes unknown to the people around thee and thou shall be made a ruler over the tribe that thou belongs unto (even that of Benjamin) and thou art faithful thou shall live to see the winding up scene &c Amen."

Continued preaching among the saints. Presided over the Mottram Branch about 12 months, then came back to Stalybridge and acted as first councilor to Pres't G. Connell for about 12 months. I was also Pres't of the No. 1 ward of the same branch, President of the Sunday School, and leader of the choir until the 25th of May 1856 when I sailed from Liverpool for Boston on board the packet ship <u>Horizon</u> with 864 saints on board, Edward Martin, President.[51] We anchored in the Bay of Mass.[achuesetts] on the 28th of June after a very favourable voyage. We had 5 deaths and 5 births. We took car at Boston for Iowa City on the 2nd July and got there on the 8th, a distance of 1700 miles.[52] We had 2 deaths on the way. We passed through Albany, Buffalo, Cleveland, Toledo, Chicago, Rock Island &c; camped at Iowa 2 weeks, then started with our hand carts to Florence.[53] Got there in 24 days, a distance of 300 miles.

---

[51] The ship, *Horizon*, chartered by the church, carried the last large company of Latter-day Saint emigrants from England, and departed Liverpool May 25, 1856, and arrived in Boston on June 28, 1856. During the crossing there were four marriages, four births, and five deaths. See Andrew D. Olsen, *The Price We Paid: The Extraordinary Story of the Willie and Martin Handcart Pioneers* (Salt Lake City: Deseret Book, 2006), 219, 221.

[52] After arriving in Boston, the majority traveled by train for eight days through Albany, Buffalo, Cleveland, Toledo, Chicago and Rock Island, Illinois. They arrived in Iowa City on July 8, 1856, which was the end of the rail line, 12 days after the Willie Handcart Company had arrived and both companies were in Iowa City until the Willie Company left on July 15. See Olsen, *The Price We Paid*, 227, 230.

[53] "Nebraska." G. Homer Durham, in MS 7644, footnote 18, 15. Florence, Territory of Nebraska, was the final stopping-off point before the trek west. Located in

Met James Bradshaw, captain of the steam ferry boat across the Missouri River. Took us in and treated us like his own. Wanted me to stay with him through the winter and he would fit me up with a team in the spring to cross the Plains with. He said it was too late to cross the Plains that season.[54] Stayed with him 1 week. His wife was also very kind to us. We left Florence on the 23rd of August 1856.[55] Arrived in Salt Lake City on Sunday November 30th about 1 o'clock noon. We had a pleasant journey until we got to Laramie when it began to be cold and provisions scarce. Traveled along very slow. On the 8th of October we crossed the river Platte for the last time. We had a very heavy, heavy hail storm that day and the river was very high and the water very cold. It was all I could do to stand it. My woman[56] and her sister Eliza[57] crossed it sticking hands[58] or they could not have

---

present-day Florence, Nebraska, Winter Quarters was one of the main settlements established by Latter-day Saints after their exodus from Nauvoo in 1846.

[54] "A 'well-finished, ironed and painted' handcart cost $20. A 'more primitive style, and without iron' cost only $10. Wagons averaged $90, and oxen to pull them averaged about $70 a yoke, with three yoke required to pull a full wagon. A wagon outfit, then, could cost $300." Olsen, *The Price We Paid*, 29.

[55] "According to the handcart plan, the emigrants would pull light-weight two wheeled carts that had shallow boxes on top, about three feet wide by five feet long, for carrying their belongings. Five people would typically be assigned to each cart, and each of them would be allowed 17 pounds of personal belongings. The weight of the handcart itself would be 60 to 75 pounds, so the total weight, with luggage, would generally be about 160 pounds . . . ." Olsen, *The Price We Paid*, 25. "For the Martin company, September's journey across Nebraska was more difficult than August's across Iowa. One reason is that the handcarts were heavier, each loaded with 100 [additional] pounds of flour and some carrying tents." Olsen, *The Price We Paid*, 295.

[56] Mary Morton Durham

[57] Eliza Morton

[58] Sticking hands together, i.e., holding hands.

stood up in it at all. All the sick that could walk at all had to get out of the wagons and walk through the river, some of them falling down in the river several times, not being able to stand up in it being so weak. Camp crossed and traveled about 1 mile and then camped. About midnight it commenced snowing and continued until sundown the next day. We traveled about 5 miles and camped. Snow about 12 inches deep. Stayed there 5 days. Buried some 12 persons while we stayed, Brother and Sister Pusil[59] among the number. Traveled on about 12

---

[59] Samuel and Margaret Pucell. "Samuel and Margaret Pucell were among the 135 to 150 members of the Martin company that died along the trail. They were converted to the Mormon faith in England and with their two daughters, Maggie, age 14, and Nellie, 9 . . . . Along the difficult trek Margaret became sick; Samuel compassionately placed his feeble wife in the family cart and continued the journey. At one of several river crossings, however, Samuel stumbled and fell, immersing himself in the cold water. His clothing froze, and within a few days he died from starvation and exposure. Tragically, Margaret died five days later, leaving Nellie and Maggie orphans on the trail. Those immigrants who were still alive when help arrived were desperately cold or numb from the early winter freeze. Ephraim Hanks, one of the rescue party, recalled reaching several travelers 'whose extremities were frozen.' 'Many such I washed with water and castile soap, until the frozen parts would fall off,' he wrote, 'after which I would sever the shreds of flesh from the remaining portions of the limbs with my scissors.' Both Pucell girls were found in similar circumstances with badly frozen feet and legs. Upon removal of the girls' shoes and socks, frozen flesh came off; Nellie's legs were particularly bad and had to be amputated. Rescuers performed the operation without anesthetic, using the only available instruments, a butcher knife and carpenter's saw. Due to the primitive surgical conditions the wound healed poorly, and bones protruded from the end of Nellie's stumps. She spent the rest of her life waddling on her knees in constant pain. At age 24 Nellie moved to Cedar City and not long thereafter became the plural wife of William Unthank. She bore six children and lived in poverty. She was, however, accustomed to facing challenges and did all in her power to make the most of her situation. Even while living in a log cabin she kept her home immaculately clean. She regularly dampened and scraped the dirt floor, making it smooth as pavement. To help meet her family's needs she took in laundry, knitted stockings to sell, carded wool, and crocheted table pieces. At times, however, she could not provide all the essentials for her children and received assistance from her Mormon bishop. As repayment for this aid and out of deeply felt gratitude, she and her children yearly

miles through the snow and camped. Both wagon trains camped along with us. Concluded to stay here until we heard something from the city. Weighed up our provisions and found we had enough to last us 8 days full rations. So we all agreed to go on half rations. That would be 8 oz. of flour per day and no groceries. Stayed 5 days. About sundown of the 5th day Joseph A. Young, Brother Gurr and Jones came into camp with the good news that there was lots of flour some 60 miles ahead, which caused us all to rejoice. Traveled on the next morning.[60]

---

scrubbed and washed the church where they worshiped each Sunday. Nellie spent most of her life in similar quiet acts of service, not only for her church but also for her family and neighbors. In 'patience and serenity' Nellie touched the lives of all with whom she associated. She died at age 69 in Cedar City. As a fitting tribute to Nellie's memory a life-size bronze likeness by noted Utah sculptor Jerry Anderson was dedicated August 13, 1991, on the campus of Southern Utah University. The Utah Legislature officially set the day aside as a 'day of praise' for Nellie Unthank, and a host of dignitaries paid tribute to her tenacity, sacrifice, and noble pioneering spirit. Perhaps Norman Bangerter, then governor of Utah, said it best when he praised Nellie as 'one of the true heroines of Utah history.'" W. Paul Reeve, "A Nine-Year Old Girl Triumphed Over the Handcart Tragedy," *History Blazer*, http://historytogo.utah.gov/utah_chapters/pioneers_and_cowboys/agirltriumphedover handcarttragedy.html (accessed Oct. 25, 2008).

[60] "After the completion of the transcontinental railroad in 1869, immigrants traveling by steam-powered ships and trains could make the trip from Liverpool, England, to Salt Lake City in just over three weeks. Earlier, the journey by ship and wagon often took nearly six months." Richard L. Jensen and William G. Hartley, "Immigration and Emigration," *Encyclopedia of Mormonism*, ed. Daniel H. Ludlow (New York: Macmillan, 1992), 674. "A week after the departure of the Martin Company, Franklin D. Richards, an apostle who had organized the handcart effort as president of the European Mission, also departed Florence with sixteen other returning missionaries. This party, on horseback and in fast carriages, passed the Martin Company on September 7, the Willie Company on September 12, and arrived in Salt Lake City on October 4. Richard's report that many more immigrants were coming was a shock: the late-starting immigrants would not be adequately clothed for the cold weather they would surely experience; they, like those in all previous lightly supplied handcart companies, would be perilously short of food; and, as they were unexpected, the last resupply wagons, which were routinely dispatched into the

mountains to meet immigrant companies, had already returned. Anticipating the worst, President Young mobilized men and women gathered for general conference and immediately ordered a massive rescue effort. A party of twenty-seven men, led by George D. Grant, left on October 7 with the first sixteen of what ultimately amounted to 200 wagons and teams. Several of the rescue party, including Grant, had been among the missionaries who had ridden in from the East five days before. Two weeks later, one of the earliest blizzards on record struck just as both handcart companies and the independent wagon companies were entering the Rocky Mountains in central Wyoming. After several days of being lashed by the fierce blizzard, people in the exposed handcart companies began to die. Grant's rescue party found the Willie Company on October 21—in a blinding snowstorm on day after they had run out of food. But the worst still lay ahead, when, after a day of rest and replenishment, the company had to struggle over the long and steep eastern approach to South Pass in the teeth of a northerly gale. Beyond the pass, the company, now amply fed and free to climb aboard empty supply wagons as they became available, moved quickly, arriving in Salt Lake City, on November 9 . . . . Those of the Martin Company . . . suffered even more. When the storm hit in October 19, they made camp and spent nine days on reduced rations waiting out the storm. Grant's party, after leaving men and supplies with the Willie Company, plunged further east through the snow with eight wagons in search of the Martin Company. A scouting party sent out ahead of the wagons found them 150 miles east of South Pass. The company, already in desperate condition, was ordered to break camp immediately. The supply wagons met them on the trail, but the provisions were not nearly enough and, after struggling 55 miles farther, the company once again went into camp near Devil's Gate to await the arrival of supplies. In the meantime, the rescue effort began to disintegrate. Rescue teams held up several days by the raging storm turned back, fearing to go on and rationalizing that the immigrant trains and Grant's advance party had either decided to winter over or had perished in the storm. The Martin Company remained in camp for five days. When no supplies came, the company, now deplorably weakened, was again forced out on the trail. It had suffered fifty-six dead before being found, and it was now losing people at an appalling rate. Relief came barely in time. A messenger ordered back west by Grant reached and turned around some of the teams that had abandoned the rescue. At least thirty wagons reached the Martin Company just as it was about to attempt the same climb to South Pass that had so sorely tested the Willie Company. Starved, frozen, spent, their spirits crushed, and many unable to walk, the people had reached the breaking point. But now warmed and fed, with those unable to walk riding in the wagons, the company moved rapidly on . . . . The Martin Company . . . finally arrived in Salt Lake City on November 30 . . . . The decision to send out the Willie and Martin companies so late in the season was extremely reckless. In mid-

April 5<sup>th</sup> 1860 – Married one of Bro. W.C. Mitchell's widows (named Mary) with 4 children, 3 boys & one girl. Bro. Amasa Lyman[61] sealed her to me for time.[62]

---

November President Brigham Young angrily reproved those who had authorized the last start or who had not ordered the several parties back to Florence when they still had the opportunity . . . . Though terrible, the suffering could have been far worse. Had the rescue effort not been launched immediately—well before the storm struck—the handcart companies would probably have been totally destroyed." Howard A. Christy, "Handcart Companies," *Encyclopedia of Mormonism*, 571-573. "The Willie and Martin companies have become history signatures of the entire handcart migration. The tragic circumstances that engulfed them and the heroic rescue mission that saved them are extraordinary incidents in the history of the western trail. Some have concluded that this plan to bring the 'poor saints from Europe' was ill advised and reckless considering the tragedy that befell these two companies. Their suffering was indeed acute and their death toll enormously high, numbering more than two hundred, but it is also remarkable that nearly eight hundred of their number survived the same extremities of cold, hunger, and privation." Carol Cornwall Madsen, *Journey to Zion: Voices from the Mormon Trail* (Salt Lake City: Deseret Book Company, 1997), 585. "In hundreds of newspapers and magazines appeared grossly exaggerated descriptions of this disaster, of which the following, taken from the *Or. Statesman*, June 15, 1857, may serve as a specimen: 'Of the 2,500 persons who started from the frontier, only about 200 frost-bitten, starving, and emaciated beings lived to tell the tale of their sufferings. The remaining 2,300 perished on the way of hunger, cold, and fatigue.'" Herbert, Howe Bancroft, *History of Utah 1540-1886*, Vol XXVI (San Francisco: The History Company, 1889), 428.

[61] Amasa M. Lyman (1813-1877) was ordained an elder in 1832 by Joseph Smith, Jr. and ordained an apostle by Brigham Young in 1842 to replace Orson Pratt in the Quorum of the Twelve Apostles, who had been suspended until 1843. When Elder Pratt returned, Lyman was removed from that quorum and placed into the First Presidency. He was later removed from the Quorum of the Twelve in 1867 and excommunicated in 1870 for preaching false doctrine. He died in 1877 and his blessings were restored in 1909.

[62] "Mary Morton Durham had no children." G. Homer Durham, in MS 7644, footnote 20, 16. (This is G. Homer Durham's reference to Thomas Durham's first wife, whom he married in 1849.) In 1860 he married Mary Moore Mitchell, widow of William Mitchell, who was accidentally killed while logging in Parowan Canyon.

Dec. 6th 1861 she bore me a Daughter which named Mary Ann.[63]

Ordained to be a Seventy in the 69th Quorum by Silas S. Smith[64] Feb'y 22nd 1865 at Parowan, Utah.

From this union there was born one daughter, Mary Ann, his first child; his first wife being without children. To see photograph of Mary Moore Mitchell and her children, see Addendum No. 4.

[63] Mary Ann Durham is the first child of Thomas Durham. "Mary Ann Durham became the wife of Hanson Bayles and moved to the San Juan country. She was the half-sister to my father, George Henry Durham (1883-1974)." G. Homer Durham, in MS 7644, footnote 21, 16. Mary Ann Mitchell Durham (b. Dec. 6, 1861, Paragonah, Iron, UT; d. Jan. 31, 1881; died Bluff, San Juan, UT; buried Bluff Cemetery, Bluff, UT. Spouse: Ole Hanson Bayles). See Utah Burials, Utah State History, http://history/utah.gov/apps/burials (accessed Oct. 25, 2008). See Addendum No. 4.

[64] Silas S. Smith (1830-1910), cousin to George A. Smith, would eventually be the leader of the famous Hole-in-the-Rock Expedition in southern Utah in 1880, called by President John Taylor to settle the San Juan area. "Taylor charged the group to establish a colony that would cultivate better relations with the Indians, deprive a white outlaw element of a refuge from the law, and expand Mormon control into the area . . . . To facilitate matters, local church leadership dispatched a thirty-man exploring party (also accompanied by two women and eight children) to determine the best route into the area. In October 1879, elements of the 230-person expedition, under the direction of Silas Smith, got underway . . . ." Robert S. McPherson, *A History of San Juan County: In the Palm of Time* (Salt Lake City: Utah State Historical Society [and] San Juan County Commission, 1995), 97-98. See also Lou Jean S. Wiggins, comp., "History of Iron County," *Pioneer Pathways* (Salt Lake City: International Society Daughters of Utah Pioneers, Talon Printing, 2002), 5:11. He was released from the San Juan Mission in 1882 and was reassigned to Manassa, Colorado. His final residence was Layton, Utah. See also Barbara Thompson Dorigatti, comp., "History of San Juan County," *Pioneer Pathways* (Salt Lake City: International Society Daughters of Utah Pioneers, Talon Printing, 2001), 4:372-373.

Married Caroline Mortensen[65] October 4, 1867.    George Q. Cannon officiated at the Endowment House, Great Salt Lake City.[66]

[65] Caroline Mortensen, born May 16, 1850, Haarbolle, Fanefjord, Praesto, Denmark, died August 19, 1915, Parowan, Iron, Utah, was the youngest of nine children born to Peder (by profession, a cooper—one who makes barrels or casks—and also a shoemaker) and Helena (Lena) Mortensen. She traveled at the age of six with her parents (ages 50 and 48) and six siblings: Anne Kirstene (called Stena) (24), Anders J. (22), Hans Jorgen (19), Lars (13), Mette Kirstene (variant spellings include Mettie Kerstina) (11) and Maria (or Mary) (9) from Copenhagen on the steamship *Rhoda*, along with 161 other emigrating Saints bound for Utah, under the leadership of Elder Johan A. Ahmanson, departing Apr. 23, 1856, to Kiel (Germany), by Railroad to Hamburg, by steamer to Grimsby in England and then by railroad to Liverpool. They sailed from Liverpool on the ship *Thornton*. See Immigrant Ships Transcribers Guild: *Ship Thornton, From Liverpool, England to New York, June 15, 1856, District of New York, Port of New York*, National Archives and Records Administration, Film M237, Reel 163, Transcribed by Sheila Jensen Tate, Mar. 31, 1999, See Immigrant Ships Transcribers Guild, "Ship Thornton," http://www.immigrantships. net/ 1800/thornton18560615_2.html   (accessed Nov. 22, 2008). It lists the family as passengers numbering 463-471 in the "Lower Between Deck" and lists the children with the surname Peterson. (The children's surname was changed to Mortensen after immigrating.) It set sail on May 4, 1856, carrying an additional 600 Saints from Great Britain—764 total members of the church. It arrived in New York City on June 14, 1856.  See Andrew Jensen, *History of the Scandinavian Mission*, 1927, 112. After arriving in New York, the emigrants had to travel 1,200 miles to Iowa City over 11 days. See Olsen, *The Price We Paid*, 7,11,12. She, along with her family, then crossed the plains with the James G. Willie Company, the fourth handcart company, which consisted of about 500 individuals, 100 handcarts and 5 wagons that departed Iowa City, Iowa July 15, 1856 and arrived in the Salt Lake Valley November 9, 1856 (just three weeks before the arrival of the Martin Company.) In spite of the heroic rescue, 68 of the company died. "One faithful Danish couple was Peder Mortensen, age 48, and his wife, Lena Mortensen, age 46, who were converted to the gospel in 1855. Due to a desire to gather to Zion and rejection by their community, they sold everything they owned in anticipation of their journey. They had land and animals. Together with their 8 children, ages 5 through 27, they traveled to Copenhagen, Denmark, to stay at the mission home until they could emigrate to Utah. The Mortensens' oldest son, Morten, was asked by the mission president to stay in Denmark and serve as a missionary. Morton, along with the rest

On the 12th of Dec. 1869 she had a son which called Tho[mas] Thompson [Durham].[67] March 14th 1869 Pres't George A. Smith[68]

---

of the Mortensen family, was concerned, but all agreed. The mission president promised the Mortensens that every one of them would reach Zion in safety because of Morten's willingness to stay and serve, along with the family's willingness to do without his much-needed help. Peder was physically disabled. He and his wife had planned to buy a wagon so that he could ride in it to the Salt Lake Valley. However, after hearing the counsel of their church leaders, they shared their money with other members of the company so that sufficient handcarts and supplies could be bought in Iowa City. Peder's disability kept him from walking. He rode in s supply wagon until about September 6, when the loads were adjusted due to a buffalo stampede. He had to be carried in a handcart from that point, until the company was rescued. Morten came to Utah after his three-year mission in 1858, two years after the rest of his family had all safely arrived in Zion." Paul D. Lyman, *The Willie Handcart Company* (Provo, Utah: BYU Studies, 2006), 62. The Mortensens said that "rawhide was taken from the carts and scraped and boiled and used as soup. Each day took its toll of strength and lives. One extremely cold day fourteen were buried in one grave. The Pedersen [Mortensen] boys helped dig the grave. (They were some of the few with the strength necessary) and the mother [and] Stene [Anna Kirstene] helped prepare the burial clothes which consisted of old and worn blankets. This was a sad day. The flour was doled out by the ounce and was guarded as a matter of life and death. One night father Peder had retired, putting his family's portion under his head. He awoke when he felt someone feeling to take it. He rose on his elbows and said, 'If you steal one morsel of food from the mouths of my hungry children, you shall not live to reach Zion.' The poor man did not; he froze to death that very night." "Mortensen Family History," MS 15877, photocopy of typescript, Church History Library, The Church of Jesus Christ of Latter-day Saints, Salt Lake City, 6-7.

[66] Salt Lake Endowment House Records, Church History Library, The Church of Jesus Christ of Latter-day Saints, Salt Lake City, GS #1,149,515, p.61. Marriage ceremony performed by George Q. Cannon with W. W. Phelps and H. W. Lawrence as witnesses.

[67] Thomas Thompson Durham, born Dec. 12, 1869; died Dec. 25, 1946.

[68] George A. Smith was a member of the 2,000-mile Zion's Camp march of 1834. He was ordained a Seventy in 1835 by Joseph Smith, Jr. and at age 21 (1839) was ordained an Apostle and a member of the Quorum of the Twelve. Future President of the Church Wilford Woodruff was ordained an apostle that same day. They replaced Thomas B. Marsh and Orson Hyde. After the church's relocation to Utah, he led a group in 1851 to colonize the area now known as Parowan. In 1868 Smith replaced

ordained me to be a High Priest and set me apart as one of the high council of the Parowan Stake of Zion, which was organized into a stake on the above day. Joseph F. Smith,[69] Erastus Snow,[70] and Bishop Dame[71] also assisted in my ordination.

---

Heber C. Kimball as First Counselor in Brigham Young's First Presidency and remained in that position until his death in 1875. His grandson, George Albert Smith, served as eighth president of the church.

[69] Joseph F. Smith, was ordained an Apostle at age 27 (1861) and became Church President in 1902 and served until his death in 1918. Smith served an additional mission to Hawaii (1884-1887) to avoid in part government prosecution for polygamy. Many church leaders, including President John Taylor, went into the "underground" to escape the authorities. One of Elder Smith's plural wives happened to be the niece of President Taylor.

[70] Erastus Fairbanks Snow (1818 – 1888), was among the first company to enter the Salt Lake Valley. He was called and ordained by Brigham Young to be an Apostle in 1849 at the age of 30 and served until his death in 1888 at age 69.

[71] William H. Dame (1819-1884) was baptized in 1841 and moved to Nauvoo, Illinois, and worked on the Nauvoo temple. In 1846 he and his wife began their journey west and arrived in 1848. He held many positions in Parowan, including mayor. See Wiggins, *Pioneer Pathways* 5:86-87. Dame, with others, laid out the township of Cedar City and Parowan. On May 12, 1852, Brigham Young organized the Iron County Stake and Dame was called to be president. On March 14, 1869 it was reorganized into the Parowan Stake (including the wards in Parowan, Paragonah, Summit, and Cedar City) and Dame continued to be stake president. In 1874 Dame was indicted and arrested along with others (including John D. Lee) for participation in the Mountain Meadows massacre. He was imprisoned for two years while authorities sought evidence. Dame later served as Bishop and in 1877 Brigham Young let Dame carry on as stake leader after a public opposition was expressed over Dame's replacement during his absence. A vote was taken which showed a split in the results and Brigham Young sided with Dame. See Seegmiller, *A History of Iron County,* 270-271. "One of the nine men indicted for the massacre. As the senior militia officer in southern Utah, he originally directed [Isaac C.] Haight not to attack the emigrants. During the early hours of Thursday, September 10, however, he consented to their death. He argued with Haight after the massacre over how the killings would be reported to authorities." Ronald W. Walker, Richard E. Turley Jr., and Glen M. Leonard, *Massacre at Mountain Meadows: An American Tragedy* (New York: Oxford University Press, 2008), 212-213, 257. See also David L. Bigler and

October 11<sup>th</sup> 1871 Caroline bore a son at ½ after 6 o'clock in the morning. At 8 o'clock Bro. Dame blessed him and named him John, died next day."[72]

Song: *THOU HAS LEARNED*[73]

---

Will Bagley, eds. *Innocent Blood: Essential Narratives of the Mountain Meadows Massacre*, Vol. 12 of *Kingdom in the West* (Norman, OK: Arthur H. Clark Co., 2008), 32-35.

[72] "John Durham died a day or so later." G. Homer Durham, in MS 7644, footnote 23, 17. The children from this union are as follows: Thomas Thompson Durham (b. Dec. 12, 1869, d. Dec. 25, 1946); John Durham, referred to above in the Journal as dying the day following his birth (b. Oct. 11, 1871, d. Oct. 12, 1871); Alfred Morton Durham (b. Sept. 23, 1872, d. Oct. 23, 1957); Lena Isabella Durham (b. Mar. 12, 1875, d. Sept. 18, 1969); Caroline Mamie Durham (b. Mar. 9, 1877, d. June 19, 1962); Sarah Anna Durham (b. June 6, 1879, d. Jan. 15, 1967); Mettie Eliza Durham (b. July 14, 1881, d. May 21, 1971); George Henry Durham (b. Sept. 12, 1883, d. Feb. 17, 1974); Alice Mary Durham (b. Feb. 8, 1885, d. Apr. 24, 1941); Wilford Mortensen Durham (b. July 1, 1890, d. Aug. 20, 1968).

[73] "The following page in his journal contains this poem. Whether he composed it, I do not know. It may have some sentimental reference to his parting with W.C. Mitchell's widow, Mary, who went to San Juan and took their daughter Mary Ann Durham in what my father, [George Henry Durham (1883-1974)] when I asked, always called 'a peaceful parting.' But the facts do not fit! Especially the last line. It may therefore have been a popular verse of the day that he wanted to preserve." G. Homer Durham, MS 7644, annotation, 17. Additional information has become available since G. Homer Durham's entry above. "A song entitled 'Thou Hast Learned to Love Another,' was published in 1849 (Spaeth, *History of Popular Music*, p. 594). In Ditson's *Home Melodist* (1859, p.38) the same title is credited to Charles Slade. Randolph (IV, 249), however, says this song is 'evidently a derivative' of 'Now Go and Leave Me If You Wish,' for a copy of which see Spaeth (*Weep Some More, My Lady*, p. 32). Though keeping the central theme, the song has undergone wide change, as can be seen from an examination of Randolph's nine

Thou hast learned to love another
    Thou hast broken every vow
We have parted from each other
    And my heart is lonely now.

I have taught my looks to shun thee
    When coldly we have met
For another's smile have won thee
    And thy voice I must forget.

Oh is it well to sever
    This heart from thine forever
Can I forget thee never
    Farewell, farewell, forever.

We have met in scenes of pleasure
    We have met in halls of pride
I have seen thy new found treasure
    I have gazed upon thy Bride.

---

texts....' Ray B. Brown, *The Alabama Folk Lyric: A Study in Origins and Media of Dissemination,* (Bowling Green University Popular Press, 1979) 142-144.

Song: *KIND FRIENDS ARE NEAR HER*[74]

1st Verse

Sleep noble hero let no one fear
Steal o'er thy brave heart as death draws near
For in her sorrow Mother will find
True hearts around her loving and kind.

Though you have left her weeping for you,
Kind friends are near her constant and true.
They'll surely cheer her when you are gone.
They will not see her mourning alone.

2nd Verse

Angels will guide her by night and day
Gently they'll lead her up through the war[75]
Though friends forsake her, they will be there
Ready to save her from dark despair.

Should angels leave her, still there is one
Who will receive her when all are gone.
One who will guide her safe to that home

---

[74] "Here is another [song]." G. Homer Durham, in MS 7644, annotation, 18. This song, published during the Civil War and associated with the Union side, was composed by B. Frank Waters, with lyrics by Ednor Rossiter, with the full title of "Kind Friends Are Near Her," An Answer to "Who Will Care For Mother Now!" (Philadelphia: Lee & Walker, 1864, M1640.W). See "Kind Friends Are Near Her," American Song Sheets, Rare Book, Manuscript, and Special Collections Library, Duke University, Duke University Libraries Digital Collections, http://library.duke.edu/digitalcollections/songsheets.bsvg301319/ (accessed March 26, 2009).

[75] The original printed lyric reads "through the way."

Where no more sorrow ever can come.

Chorus [sung after each verse][76]

Friends will be near her,
Angels will come,
To guard and cheer her,
When you are gone.

---

[76] The chorus was not included in Thomas Durham's Journal, but is added here.

Song: *HARD TIMES*[77]

---

[77] "Followed on the next page by 'Hard Times Come Again No More,' which his Parowan Ward choir sang for General Wm. T. Sherman in Salt Lake City, and melted his feelings towards 'the Mormons.'" G. Homer Durham, MS 7644, annotation, 18. This song was composed by the pre-eminent songwriter in the United States of the 19th Century, Stephen Collins Foster (1826-1864), known as the "father of American music." His songs include "Oh! Susanna," "Camptown Races," "My Old Kentucky Home," "Beautiful Dreamer," etc., and remain popular today. "Hard Times Come Again No More" was written in 1854 (New York: Firth, Pond & Co.) It was well known and popular in its day both in American and Europe and was a favorite of both sides of the Civil War. The handwritten lyrics vary from the composer's original lyrics. It is possible that along with this song, the previous song in his journal, "Kind Friends Are Near Her," was also sung by the choir on this occasion. "Hard Times" enjoys popularity to this day and has been sung by contemporary artists such as James Taylor, Bob Dylan, Johnny Cash and Bruce Springsteen. According to pioneer Joseph Fish, "On the morning of the 25th of September, 1870, seventeen wagons left Parowan en route to Salt Lake City. It was a regular caravan of singers, who were like one big happy family, as they jolted along over the rough, rocky roads, singing songs and telling stories of their journey across the plains and from foreign lands across the ocean in sailing vessels. Then at night they'd sing and dance around the campfire while someone played the violin. In the group were Lars Mortensen and wife Cornelia, Peter M. Jenson and wife Mary M. Jenson, Hans Mortensen, Joseph Fish and wife Mary, Andrew Mortensen, Josephine Smith, William Wilcock, Thomas Evans, Jenkin Evans, Smith D. Rogers and wife Aunt Eliza, John Eyre and wife Lizzie Benson, Ellen Marsden, Mary Ann Durham, William C. Mitchell, Huldah and Mary Ann Mitchell, James Connell, Sarah Ann Adams, Emma Morris, Lizzie Morris, Caroline Durham. Morgan Richards, Jr. and Margaret Adams were in the company going to be married, in the Old Endowment House and grandmother Mary Ann Adams, Sarah D. Morris, and her daughter Mary Ann Morris Rasmussen and baby John T. Rasmussen were in the Richards outfit." See Dalton, *Iron County Mission*, 295-296. ("Morgan Richards and Margaret Adams were married about 5 o'clock, 3rd October, 1870, in the Endowment House, by Apostle Wilford Woodruff. Among those present and officiating, were Joseph F. Smith, Samuel H. B. Smith, John Lyon, W. W. Phelps, Bathsheba W. Smith and John D. T. McCallister, President of the ST. George Stake." Dalton, *Iron County Mission*, 296.

[Stephen Foster's original lyrics]:
*HARD TIMES COME AGAIN NO MORE*
Let us pause in life's pleasures and count its many tears
While we all sup sorrow with the poor:
There's a song that will linger forever in our ears;
Oh! Hard Times, come again no more.

Chorus:

'Tis the song, the sigh of the weary;
Hard Times, Hard Times, come again no more:
Many days you have lingered around my cabin door;
Oh! Hard Times, come again no more.

While we seek mirth and beauty and music light and gay
There are frail forms fainting at the door:
Though their voices are silent, their pleading looks will say
Oh! Hard Times, come again no more.

(Chorus)

There's a pale drooping maiden who toils her life away
With a worn heart whose better days are o'er:
Though her voice would be merry, 'tis sighing all the day
Oh! Hard Times, come again no more.

(Chorus)

'Tis a sigh that is wafted across the troubled wave,
'Tis a wail that is heard upon the shore,
'Tis a dirge that is murmured around the lowly grave
Oh! Hard Times, come again no more.

(Chorus)
See Stephen Foster Memorial (Foster Hall Collection, Center for American Music, University of Pittsburgh Library System), http://www.pitt.edu/~amerimus/lyrics. htm#Hard%20Times%20 Come%20Again%20No%20More (accessed Mar. 29, 2009).

Song: *HARD TIMES*

1st Verse

Let us pause in life's pleasures
And count its many tears.
While we sip sorrow with the poor
'Tis a song that will linger forever in our ears.
Oh, hard times come again no more.

Chorus

2nd Verse

There's a pale drooping maiden
Who toils her life away
With a worn heart who's better days are over.
Tho her heart would be merry
'Tis sighing all the day.
Oh, hard times come again no more.

Chorus

'Tis the song, the sigh of the weary.
Hard times, hard times come again no more.
Many days you have lingered around my cabin door.

End of Journal

## *Addendum No. 1*

Photograph of Thomas Durham and sons [Caroline Mortensen, mother]

*Left to Right*: Thomas Thompson Durham, Alfred Morton Durham, George Henry Durham, Wilford Mortensen Durham
Seated: Thomas Durham
Picture taken ca. 1904-1908.
Photographer unknown; not part of a collection.
Original in possession of Paul D. Durham.

## *Addendum No. 2*

Photograph of Caroline Mortensen Durham and daughters[1]
[Thomas Durham, father]

*Standing Left to Right*: Mettie Eliza Durham (Mickelson, Robinson), Sarah Anna Durham (Connell), Lena Isabella Durham (McGregor), Caroline Mamie Durham (Orton), Alice Mary Durham, *Seated*: Caroline Mortensen Durham
Picture taken ca. 1904-1908.
Photographer unknown; not part of a collection.
Copy of original photograph taken by Paul D. Durham while in possession of Vera Durham Williams, ca. 1978.

---

[1] Identities of the daughters were determined by Richards Durham and Vera Durham Williams (A. Richards Durham, letter to author, May 21, 1982, MS), although one researcher shows them identified left to right by age. See Fredrick Parley Jones and Mary Jones, *The Peder Mortensen and Helena Sandersen Family* (Aurora, CO: The Wright Place, 2007), 1633, available in *The Peder Mortensen and Helena Sandersen Family*, CD-ROM no. 3957, Family History Library, The Church of Jesus Christ of Latter-day Saints, Salt Lake City.

## *Addendum No. 3*

Photograph of Thomas Durham and Caroline Mortensen Family

*Back Row*: Lena Isabella Durham (McGregor), Thomas Thompson Durham, Alfred Morton Durham, Caroline Mamie Durham (Orton), Sarah Anna Durham (Connell), *Front Row*: Wilford Mortensen Durham, seated on lap, Thomas Durham, George Henry Durham, Mettie Eliza Durham (Mickelson), Alice Mary Durham, Caroline Mortensen Durham.
Picture taken ca. 1891.
Photographer unknown; not part of a collection.
Photograph in Luella Adams Dalton, comp., *History of Iron County Mission,* 54.

*Addendum No. 4*

Photograph of Mary Moore Mitchell Durham [Thomas Durham's second wife] and her children, including Mary Ann Durham, first child, of Thomas Durham.

*Back Row*: Elizabeth M. Allen, Zetland Mitchell, James A. Mitchell, John M. Mitchell.
*Front Row*: Mary Ann Durham, Mary Moore Mitchell Durham
Picture taken ca. 1865-68.
Photographer unknown; not part of a collection.
Photograph in Luella Adams Dalton, comp., *History of Iron County Mission,* 62.

In 1860 Thomas married Mary Moore Mitchell, one of the widows of William Mitchell, who was accidentally killed while logging in Parowan Canyon. From this union there was born one daughter, Mary Ann, his first child; his first wife being without children.

*Addendum No. 5*

Photograph of Thomas and Caroline Mortensen Durham

Used by permission, Utah State Historical Society, Salt Lake City.
All Rights Reserved.
Utah State Historical Classified Photo Collection
Identifier 39222001346852; Photo No. 12158
Photographer unknown, paper print, 5x7 inches.
Picture taken ca. 1904-1908.
Original donated by Mrs. George H. Durham.

*Addendum No. 6*

Photographs of Alfred Morton Durham, author of "Sketch of the Life of Thomas Durham"

*Left*: Alfred Morton Durham, 1912.
Photographer unknown; not part of a collection.
Original in possession of Paul D. Durham.

*Right*: Alfred Morton Durham, ca. 1920, taken in Beaver, Utah.
Photographer unknown; not part of a collection.
Original in possession of Paul D. Durham.

## *Addendum No. 7*

Photographs of John Durham (1790-1863), Isabella Thompson Durham (1800-1883), and Sarah Durham Morris (1825-1916); father, mother and sister of Thomas Durham.

*Left*: John Durham
Photographer unknown; not part of a collection.

*Middle*: Isabella Thompson Durham
Photographer unknown; not part of a collection.

*Right*: Sarah Durham Morris
Photographer unknown; not part of a collection.

Photocopies in possession of editor.
Source: See Emma Topham and Cora Rowley, "A Sketch of the Life of Sarah Durham Morris as Remembered by her Grandaughters," [sic] (Cedar City, UT, n.p., n.d., photocopy of typescript ), 83, 86.

*Addendum No. 8*

Photograph of Mayor Thomas Durham, published 1901.

Actual date of original photograph: Unknown

Thomas Durham, "New Mayors Chosen for Utah Cities," *Deseret Evening News*, December 21, 1901, 32. "At the city election held in Parowan on November 5, Thomas Durham, Democrat, got 143 votes as against 115 for Simon A. Matheson, Republican, majority 28. Mr. Durham was born in England, May 2, 1828. At an early age he developed strong musical tendencies which have been exhibited throughout his life. He was appointed leader of the choir at Parowan in 1856 and still retains that position." It should be noted that of all the mayoral candidates that won their election that year in Utah, seventeen were Republican, fourteen were Democrat, and eleven were of the Citizen Party.

## *Addendum No. 9*

Parowan Ward Choir, (one group photographed; not entire choir) March, 1909 or June, 1912.

*Back row*: Genavive Ward, Thomas T. Durham, Caroline Mamie Durham Orton, Dr. Joseph McGregor, Florence Orton, Clayton Mitchell. *Middle Row*: Sarah Anna Durham, William H. Orton, Anna Rasmussen, George H. Durham, Ada McGregor, Walter C. Mitchell. *Front Row*: Maggie Dean Marsden, Alice Matheson, Florence Mitchell, Ida Orton, Jannie Benson.
Picture taken ca. 1912, according to Luella Adams Dalton, comp., *History of Iron County Mission,* 58, but according to Lowell M. Durham, was taken at the time of Thomas Durham's death in 1909, "General Sherman and the Parowan Choir—A Little-known Story of Music on the Mormon Frontier," *Improvement Era*, 1943, 78.

Photographer unknown; not part of a collection.

*Addendum No. 10*

Parowan Ward Choir, (another group photographed; not entire choir) March, 1909 or June, 1912.

*Back row*: Laura Gurr, Annie C. Durham, Calvin Connell, Alice Durham, William Marsden, Isa D. McGregor, Blanche Whitney, Belle Mitchell. *Middle Row*: Milton L. Ollorton, Bertha Whitney, Mahonri Decker, Loloa Ollorton, Alexander Orton, Irene Mitchell. *Front Row*: Maud Mickelson, Mettie Eliza Durham, Nellie Marsden, Augusta Dalton, Sylvia Mitchell, Lucille Adams.
Picture taken ca. 1912, according to Luella Adams Dalton, comp., *History of Iron County Mission,* 58, but according to Lowell M. Durham, was taken at the time of Thomas Durham's death in 1909, "General Sherman and the Parowan Choir—A Little-known Story of Music on the Mormon Frontier," *Improvement Era,* 1943, 78.

Photographer unknown; not part of a collection.

*Addendum No. 11*

Parowan Brass Band in Early Days

*Back row*: Jess Mortenson, Jimmy Connell, Mahonri Decker, James Connell, Cabeb Orton, Hans Mortenson. *Front Row*: Johnny Rasmussen, Ralph Wilcock, Wallace Mortenson, William Prichard.

Actual date of original photograph: Unknown
Photographer unknown; not part of a collection.
Photograph in Luella Adams Dalton, comp., *History of Iron County Mission*, 55.

*Addendum No. 12*

## Stars of Morning, Shout for Joy!

Thomas Durham

*Hymns*, (Salt Lake City: The Deseret News Press, 1948), no. 164. It had been published previously in an earlier hymnal. See *"Stars of Morning, Shout for Joy,"* *Deseret Sunday School Songs* (Salt Lake City, The Deseret News Press, 1909), no. 1.

*Addendum No. 13*

## No. 170      **Nephite Lamentation**

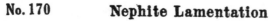

Thomas Durham, "Nephite Lamentation," *The Primary Song Book*, Including Marches and Voluntaries (Salt Lake City: General Board of Primary Associations, 1912), no. 170, arranged by H. E. Giles. Photocopy of original at Church History Library, The Church of Jesus Christ of Latter-day Saints, Salt Lake City.

## Addendum No. 14

# "O My Father"
## Tune - Nephite Lamentation

Words by Eliza R. Snow                    Thomas Durham

*"O My Father,"* transcription by Heidi Durham Berry

## *Addendum No. 15*

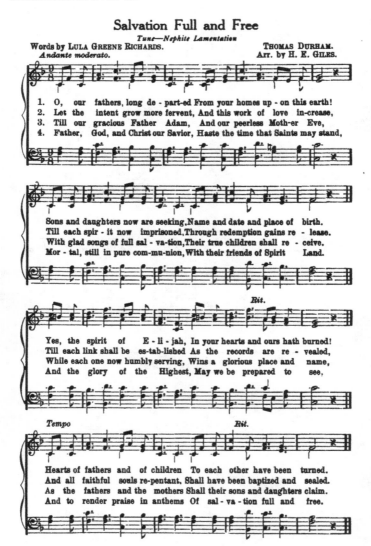

### Salvation Full and Free

*Tune—Nephite Lamentation*

Words by LULA GREENE RICHARDS.
*Andante moderato.*

THOMAS DURHAM.
Arr. by H. E. GILES.

1. O, our fathers, long de - part-ed From your homes up - on this earth!
2. Let the intent grow more fervent, And this work of love in-crease,
3. Till our gracious Father Adam, And our peerless Moth-er Eve,
4. Father, God, and Christ our Savior, Haste the time that Saints may stand,

Sons and daughters now are seeking, Name and date and place of birth.
Till each spir - it now imprisoned, Through redemption gains re - lease.
With glad songs of full sal - va-tion, Their true children shall re - ceive.
Mor - tal, still in pure com-mu-nion, With their friends of Spirit Land.

Yes, the spirit of E - li - jah, In your hearts and ours hath burned!
Till each link shall be es-tab-lished As the records are re - vealed,
While each one now humbly serving, Wins a glorious place and name,
And the glory of the Highest, May we be prepared to see,

Hearts of fathers and of children To each other have been turned.
And all faithful souls re-pentant, Shall have been baptized and sealed.
As the fathers and the mothers Shall their sons and daughters claim.
And to render praise in anthems Of sal - va -tion full and free.

Lula Greene Richards and Thomas Durham, "*Salvation Full and Free* (Hymn with Music)," *The Utah Genealogical and Historical Magazine*, July, 1922, 95-96. Digital copy, "The Utah Genealogical and Historical Magazine," Genealogical Society of Utah, Google Books, http://books.google.com/books?id=tsUUAAAAYAAJ&pg=PA96-IA3 (accessed Nov. 25, 2008).

## *Addendum No. 16*

Theodore E. Curtis and Thomas Durham, "*Hail Cumorah! Silent Wonder* (Nephite Song of Lamentation)," (Salt Lake City: Deseret Music Publishers, 1960), arranged by George H. Durham, available from Jackman Music Corp., Orem, UT. Photocopy of first page.

*Addendum No. 17*

Photocopy of Original Title Page of Thomas Durham Journal

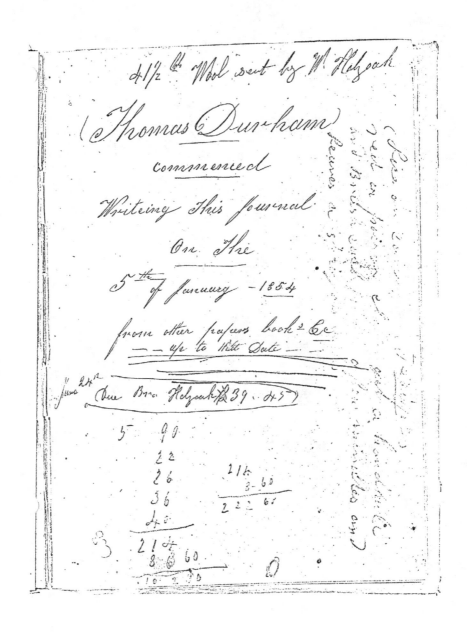

*Addendum No. 18*

Kind Friends Are Near Her

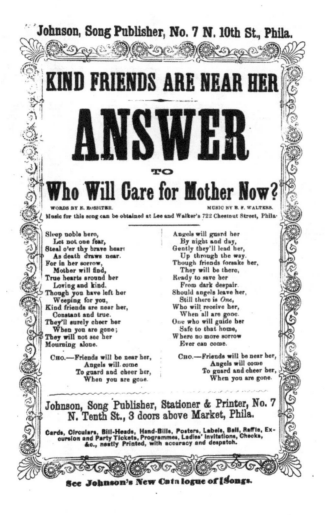

"Kind Friends Are Near Her, Answer to Who Will Care for Mother Now," *American Singing: Nineteenth Century Song Sheets,* American Memory, Library of Congress,http://memory.loc.gov/cgi-bin/query/D?amss:1:./temp/~ammem_jbO8: (accessed March 26, 2009).

## Addendum No. 19

# Hard Times Come Again No More

Text by Stephen Collins Foster

STEPHEN COLLINS FOSTER
1826-1864

Voice and Piano

Let     us    pause     in  life's plea-sures    and    count its ma – ny tears    While  we
While  we    seek    mirth and beau-ty    and    mus – ic light and  gay    There are
There's a    pale    droop-ing maid-en    who    toils her life  a – way    With   a
'Tis    a    sigh    that  is  waft-ed    a – cross the trou-bled wave,    'Tis   a

all     sup    sor-row with the poor;    There's  a    song that will lin – ger    for-
frail    forms    faint-ing  at  the door;    Though their  voic – es  are  si – lent,  their
worn heart whose bet-ter days are  o'er;    Though her  voice would be mer – ry,    'tis
wail    that is  heard up-on the shore,    'Tis    a    dirge that is mur-mured  a-

"*Hard Times Come Again No More*," Stan Sanderson, http://www.ibiblio.org/ mutopia/ cgibin/piece-info.cgi?id=371 (accessed Mar. 29, 2009). In Public Domain.

# INDEX

CPSIA information can be obtained
at www.ICGtesting.com
Printed in the USA
BVHW072052310122
627588BV00001B/54